D0699457

TEN
African
Heroes

Previous Books by Thomas Patrick Melady

The Ambassador's Story
Burundi: The Tragic Years
Catholics in the Public Square (editor)
Development: Lessons for the Future (co-author)
Faces of Africa
Faith-Family-Friends
House Divided (co-author)
Idi Amin: Hitler in Africa (co-author)
Kenneth Kaunda of Zambia
Profiles of African Leaders
Public Catholicism (editor)
Revolution of Color
Uganda: The Asian Exiles
Western Policy and the Third World
White Man's Future in Black Africa
Witness to the Faith (editor)

Previous Books by Margaret Badum Melady

The Rhetoric of Pope John Paul II
Léopold Sédar Senghor: Rhythm and Reconciliation
Poesie Vivante II

TEN
African
Heroes

**THE SWEEP OF INDEPENDENCE
IN BLACK AFRICA**

Thomas Patrick Melady
and
Margaret Badum Melady

ORBIS BOOKS
Maryknoll, New York 10545

Copyright © 2011 by Thomas Patrick Melady and Margaret Badum Melady.

Published by Orbis Books, Maryknoll, NY 10545-0302.

Queries regarding rights and permissions should be addressed to
Orbis Books, P.O. Box 302, Maryknoll, NY 10545-0302.

Manufactured in the United States of America.

Library of Congress Cataloging-in-Publication Data

Melady, Thomas Patrick.
     Ten African heroes : the sweep of independence in Black Africa /
 Thomas Patrick Melady and Margaret Badum Melady.
        p.   cm.
     Includes bibliographical references.
     ISBN 978-1-57075-929-1 (pbk.)
     1. Nationalists – Africa, Sub-Saharan – Biography. 2. Statesmen – Africa,
 Sub-Saharan – Biography. 3. Africa, Sub-Saharan – Biography. 4. Africa,
 Sub-Saharan – History – Autonomy and independence movements. 5. National
 liberation movements – Africa, Sub-Saharan.   I. Melady, Margaret Badum.
 II. Title.   III. Title: Sweep of independence in Black Africa.
 DT352.6.M45 2011
 967.03′260922 – dc22   2010035612

To our grandchildren:

Alexander Morin	*Samantha Micklos*
Nicholas Morin	*Zachary Micklos*
Julia Rey	*Katherine Micklos*

Emily Micklos

With the prayerful best wishes that their lives will be ones of service to the world family

Contents

Foreword

Individual relationships of trust form the bedrock of international relations between states. This should be axiomatic, but too often the field of international relations is assumed to be something of a mere forensic examination, the study of what happened between nations. Individual relationships matter far more than meets the eye. Individuals, not just institutions nor the majesty of a government, matter in foreign relations.

Values matter. People act upon their values not just on the basis of policies or interests. Some of the portraits of the leaders in this volume reveal deep affinities with the Catholic or Protestant faiths. The authors tie value systems into the work of individual leaders. In turn, the leaders' spiritual roots are often identified and traced through their lives and work. In some cases, a specific influence — such as the philosophy of Pierre Teilhard de Chardin — is clearly spelled out.

The influence of religion in individual lives is often neglected in the study of history, public policy, and international relations. This volume is careful to identify the impact of religion on the people and events of the time.

This work will be invaluable for anyone who seeks to understand a period of tremendous change in Africa, the "sweep of African independence in the 1960s." This period produced a large number of gifted, visionary, and passionate leaders whose lives are portrayed in this volume. These leaders exerted a tangible influence on the transformation that took place.

The authors have provided powerful sketches of the political leaders they describe, based on first-hand knowledge. Unforgettable, revealing details flow through this work. For example, there are Ambassador Melady's philosophical discussions with Léopold Sédar Senghor. There is also the image of Holden Roberto arriving in New York, suffering from a gunshot wound, trying to conceal the fact from all except the authors.

In addition, we learn that individuals can make a difference, just as Ambassador and Mrs. Melady quietly and effectively mobilized countless governmental and nongovernmental efforts to assist in the political transition taking place in Africa, while administering to the needs of the people.

Historians should be grateful for these gripping accounts of the people and events of Africa in the 1960s. Readers will enjoy the insights and detailed reflections memorialized in this volume.

Ambassador John K. Menzies
Dean of the John C. Whitehead School
of Diplomacy and International Relations
at Seton Hall University

Preface

The decade of the 1960s with its sweep of independence in black Africa initiated a significant forward movement in the march of the world community to a more just society. This decade was witness to the transfer of freedom and self-rule to the peoples in most of black Africa. It triggered the rise to a significant presence in world affairs of a major portion of the third world.

With the exception of the territories still controlled by Portugal, this decade witnessed the fading away of the nineteenth-century colonial structures and a rejection in the then still nonindependent countries in southern Africa of racial separation as advocated by the Republic of South Africa.

The Catholic Church responded to the significance of the change. Most of the dioceses in this area saw the change from white episcopal leadership to the arrival on the scene of black cardinals, archbishops, and bishops.

This sweep occurred at the height of the Cold War. More than a few experts in Afro-Asian affairs predicted that Africa would embrace the ideology of international communism then advocated by the Soviet Union. This did not occur. The convergence of African spiritual traditions, as described by Sédar Senghor, Nyerere, and Kaunda, with the spiritual values of

Christianity, as brought to black Africa by the European and American missionaries, was embraced by the African peoples.

The west coast of Africa was the home of two of the pioneer leaders in the independence movement in the 1960s. Sylvanus Olympio benefited from a tricultural background. He attended a German elementary mission school, a French lycée, and the London School of Economics, where he majored in commerce. Olympio understood the significance of living in a trusteeship country where the administering country was obligated to prepare the people for self-rule and, consequently, independence.

At around the same time, Léopold Sédar Senghor was a student in Senegal, which had a relationship with France going back to the French revolution. An obviously brilliant student, Senghor passed through the French educational system, including a university, with high honors. He was especially influenced by the philosophy of Teilhard de Chardin, which emphasized the forward movement of the human family. Both leaders, within the particular traditions of Senegal and Togo, practiced engagement and avoided the policies of confrontation.

Tom Mboya, Julius Nyerere, Seretse Khama, and Kenneth Kaunda faced the challenges not only of preparing their peoples for self-rule and independence, but also of advocating at the same time racial reconciliation. These four leaders had all felt the sting of racism. Both in West and East Africa, these leaders of the 1960s were firmly committed to their values: their goal of independence and the art of engagement over confrontation. This provided for a peaceful transition that could have otherwise been a violent one.

Ahmadou Ahidjo had the early experience of living in a multiethnic society. The Christian, Moslem, and traditional communities of Cameroon also provided for an environment that favored an administration committed to preparing for independence.

The two African revolutionary leaders of the sweep of the 1960s who did not witness the benefits of independence at the same time as the other leaders were Holden Roberto and Eduardo Mondlane. Independence for Angola and Mozambique was delayed for fifteen years as Portugal refused to join the British, French, and Belgian governments in participating in the sweep of the 1960s.

Having established the framework that led to independence, Mondlane was assassinated before he could experience the concrete results. Holden Roberto, even though not awarded the top leadership position, participated in the emergence of Angola to full independence.

William V. S. Tubman, ignored at first as a significant player in the sweep of independence in the 1960s, deserves on reexamination recognition and praise. He confronted the delicate internal challenge of a cultural gap between the small minority of Americo-Liberians and the indigenous peoples of Liberia. He articulated the critical importance of bridging the divide and made significant progress in doing that.

The sweep of change in black Africa came sooner than most authorities in the U.S. government agencies predicted. The private sector responded well because the churches — both Catholic and Protestant — had established very good people-to-people relationships in black Africa.

In the Cold War atmosphere, the black African peoples, through the swift-moving currents of the 1960s and subsequent 1970s, made their own choices, faithful to their core values. The Africa of that period rejected the communism of the 1960s and instead merged some aspects of Western civilization into their cultures.

The relationship now between the African peoples and the West is a more natural one. The fears of some in the early 1960s of significant and sustained violence between the Muslim and Christian communities in black Africa did not occur. There are a few exceptions, like in Nigeria, but they are diminishing.

Black Africa, after the sweep of independence, assisted the world community to become a more just and humane society.

Acknowledgments

Ten African Heroes was an intrinsic part of our early lives. It actually started before we met when Tom was serving in Ethiopia with the Foreign Operations Administration in 1956–57. Energized by his actual experience of working with the people of Africa, he continued his association and is deeply indebted to the small nucleus of academics and those concerned at the end of the colonial era with the future Africa. Rawson L. Wood was of significant assistance to Tom during this period. After our meeting and marriage in 1961, we were able to meet and have sustained relationships with a variety of African leaders, especially the ten included in this book. The time these leaders gave us and their patience in responding to our questions and answering our correspondence will always be appreciated.

While most of the action in this book takes place in the 1960s, it was only fifty years later when friends and people active in African affairs urged us to write this book, as it could be of interest to those studying Africa. In this regard, we appreciate the interest and encouragement from Michael Leach, publisher emeritus of Orbis Books. The two assistants in Tom's office, who participated in the preparation of the manuscript, were Casey Bassett and J. Cushman Laurent. Members of the staff of the Institute of World Politics assisted in various others ways.

The archives departments of Duquesne University and Fordham University were very helpful in researching the facts of the visits of several of the African leaders to their campuses.

Our memories of the heroic advocate of racial reconciliation, Jesuit priest John LaFarge, who urged us also to write about our experiences and beliefs, are always with us. Since then both of us have published a number of books.

Introduction

The Breakthrough to African Affairs

The one-year assignment with the Foreign Operations Administration (FOA) in Ethiopia in 1956–57 gave me the urge to become involved in African affairs. I felt that the world was at the eve of significant change and that in my lifetime colonialism in Africa would come to an end and we would see sovereign independent states. My Ph.D. was in international affairs, and my experience with FOA in Ethiopia gave me the opportunity to apply the lessons of history and diplomacy to developments in an African country. When I returned to Washington in 1957, I had hoped that I would receive an assignment in Africa, but the only one available was in Iraq. I decided to look around for other opportunities that could lead to greater involvement in African affairs. I wanted to be at the beginning of what would become the sweep of independence in black Africa.

I followed the worldwide attention to the developments in Ghana with excitement. It eventually became an independent state on March 6, 1957. This event was, for me, the beginning of a significant change. How could I become involved? As I looked for new opportunities, I found that my enthusiasm for a pending change in Africa was not shared by many of the African

1

specialists. It was pointed out to me that the two major European powers that had colonies in Africa were France and Great Britain. Empires, I was told, do not give up their territories easily. Both Belgium and Portugal had not even started the process of local communal rule.

I, however, sensed a change. French president Charles de Gaulle talked about the French-African colonies becoming part of the French Republic. Local parliamentary elections were being held in the French colonies, and those elected would represent their African constituents in the French Parliament. Winston Churchill, who had in the early 1950s pointed out that he was not named prime minister of the United Kingdom to give away British colonies, was not opposed to the granting of independence to Ghana and even encouraged the discussions concerning the future of Kenya.

In my spare time in the spring and summer of 1957, while still with the Foreign Operations Administration, I looked for opportunities to become involved in African Affairs. My several visits to New York, Philadelphia, and Chicago led to interesting possibilities for the future, but no immediate opportunities for employment. In July 1957, I dropped in to see my friend Vernon F. Gallagher, who was serving as president of Duquesne University in Pittsburgh, which was and is my alma mater. I had kept in contact with him since my graduation from Duquesne in 1950. The university was founded and administered by the Spiritan Fathers. Their primary mission was to serve in black Africa and in other parts of the third world. They came to the United States to work primarily among African Americans in the nineteenth century. While Father Gallagher was certainly interested in the possibility of an African studies program at Duquesne, he had a position that he wanted filled immediately. Several months previously, the director of development and public relations had resigned. He told me that he was looking for the "right person" who knew the history and appreciated the mission of Duquesne and at the same time could communicate its vision and direct the resource development campaign. He offered me the job.

I spent the weekend thinking about it. It was not a position that would take me directly into African matters. On the other hand, the leadership of the university was in the hands of a religious order primarily involved in Africa. I decided to accept the offer and pointed out to Father Gallagher that in addition to my primary job I would like to design a plan where there could be a program in African studies at Duquesne. My work at Duquesne started in September, and it was primarily involved with development and fundraising matters. I was able, in my last year on the staff, to develop a program of African language studies that would be incorporated into an institute of African studies offering a master's degree. But while that did in a way bring me into contact with African matters, after three years I knew I wanted more direct involvement. The study of languages was not my primary interest. While languages were important, I felt at this moment that government, economic development, and international relations should be a primary interest, as Africa was going through this historic transition at the time of the Cold War. I found many opportunities to be involved in international matters in Pittsburgh.

I learned in the spring of 1959 that the Catholic Interracial Council of New York City was studying the prospect of enlarging its activities to include a program that would assist African diplomats arriving in New York City for duty at the United Nations in obtaining places to live. There was also an interest in assisting African students in finding summer employment and part-time jobs while they were at the university. In addition, the Catholic Interracial Council believed that there would be a need to facilitate useful and appealing events that the African leaders could attend while visiting the United States. It was common knowledge that once independent, African leaders wanted to visit the United States and that the U.S. government was interested in arranging these visits.

It was the Cold War, and the Soviet-Communist media machinery took advantage of incidents where members of African delegations were treated badly in stores and other public facilities because they were black. These incidents continued to grow because the laws in most U.S. states did not prohibit discrimination in public facilities. This was one of the main reasons why the Catholic Interracial Council (CIC) was looking into the formation of another organization that could focus exclusively on these kinds of matters.

An institutional development organization, John Price Jones of New York City, contacted me and offered me a position to direct the basic overall study. Their client (the CIC) had to make the decision of whether or not I was an acceptable person to oversee the study. I was consequently invited to New York City and met Rawson L. Wood, a New York business leader and philanthropist who was serving as chairman of the board of CIC. He told me that when the new organization was in operation, he wanted me to be in charge of it. In the meantime, I needed to find employment that would support me in New York City.

John Price Jones offered me the position. The study would determine if there would be enough support for an organization that was dedicated to assisting African diplomats and African students in the area of greater New York City. I decided to take a chance. I was becoming impatient with waiting for the opportunity to become directly involved in African affairs. I had a good number of friends, both at Duquesne University and elsewhere in Pittsburgh. In many ways I regretted leaving them, but I felt that this was a new opportunity, so I grabbed it.

The study recommended that the Catholic Interracial Council set up a side organization that was separately incorporated. It would be dedicated to the assisting of African diplomats and officials living in the New York area and also help to develop a program in identifying full-time and part-time summer jobs for African students. It also would have the general purpose of promoting an interest in African relations in the United States. In November 1959, the Africa Service Institute was formally established and was recognized by the federal government as a nonprofit institution with all of the usual tax privileges. I was offered the position of president, and my primary assignment was to present a five-year plan for the organization.

The five-year plan was based on the assumption that in the first part of the 1960s there would be a tremendous rush of African officials and students coming to New York City. It would be a small operation and the basic plan was to work with organizations already in existence and to serve as a special friend for the visiting African diplomats, students, and leaders. The plan

U.S. Department of State

Thomas and Margaret Melady at home with their daughters, Christina and Monica, in October 1969, when the White House informed him of his appointment as U.S. Ambassador to Burundi.

called for five to eight years of operations. The institute lasted until 1968, when I joined the faculty of Seton Hall University. In 1969 I was appointed ambassador to Burundi. My seven years with the Africa Service Institute, teaching at St. John's and Fordham Universities, were full of memorable experiences. My first six books on Africa were written in that period. Margaret helped on many books, as well as co-authoring articles. As I transitioned to full-time academic work at Seton Hall University, Philip Scharper, editor of Sheed & Ward, having read several of our articles, invited us to co-author a book on the impact of poverty, illiteracy and disease on the world family.

The manuscript, *House Divided,* was later published by Sheed & Ward and coincided with my appointment as U.S. ambassador to Burundi. I later realized that my contacts with the leaders would continue for several decades, as they had become friends.

Recognizing the era that we were in, we were concerned that some aspects of racial prejudice existed in housing and employment. This was before the actions taken by the Supreme Court or by the Congress to correct these injustices. We undertook a plan of welcoming African leaders, when they came to the United States. Since the United Nations was of such importance to the African leaders it was apparent to us that many of the leaders would make a visit to New York City, as the United Nations was and remains a top priority. The challenge was how to show them the best face of America. It was the Cold War era and in the United States, every misstep on these matters was magnified and reported extensively in the media of third world countries.

In regard to African leaders I recommended that the new organization, Africa Service Institute, identify universities that would invite them to speak and confer upon them a high academic honor. In addition to this, we needed to take extra steps to establish that a black African head of state or government was equal to his or her European or African counterpart. The prime minister of a European country would visit and in an appropriate academic ceremony would receive the university's highest academic accolade. This was usually the doctor of laws degree. We had to recognize that the African leaders visiting the United States, having read and learned about our racial problems, would sometimes be insecure. We needed to offer them the strong hand of friendship and to take all steps to assure that their visits to us would be positive and memorable.

Since the original funding for the Catholic Interracial Council came from the Archdiocese of New York, and it was the CIC that indicated concern for how African visitors and students would be treated, I felt that the officials of the archdiocese should be briefed on our plans. I was advised to call upon Bishop James Griffiths, an auxiliary bishop of the archdiocese who was primarily responsible for international matters. Since he in many ways was the voice of the Catholic Church at the U.N., he quickly acknowledged the challenge of the large number of African officials that would be visiting New York City. He gave me a strong endorsement of the concept of an organization assisting African visitors with housing and related problems of employment for their spouses and families. A strong advocate for emphasizing the matters of racial reconciliation was Father John LaFarge. The Jesuit activist had decades of experience in fighting racial discrimination.

I realized that the change in black Africa was occurring at the time of the Cold War. While I wanted to see independent sovereign states in the place of colonies in Africa, I feared that the Soviet Union would seize this opportunity to promote the Communist Party as the dominant political system in the newly independent states.

My move to New York was completed in the fall of 1959, and I was fortunate for the first few months to enjoy the hospitality of the family of my friend Dr. George Novak. He, at that time, was serving for the Agency for International Development in Jordan. His mother was a delightful Polish lady who treated me like a grandson for the three months that I stayed there. Their apartment was located in Brooklyn Heights, and it was an easy ride to the office of John Price Jones in the Wall Street area. Our plan for the Africa Service Institute was ready for implementation in the winter of 1960. During this period I became deeply involved in African activities. This included African student groups in the New York City area and several ecumenical organizations favoring independence. I also sought academic appointments where I could focus on teaching courses related primarily to black Africa. In 1960, a group planning an African trade fair engaged me for a few months.

When it came to the implementation of a new organization separate from its original sponsor, the Catholic Interracial Council, the big challenge was the budget. With the president and two or three staff, it was estimated that we needed around $65,000 annually for the operations that would include staff, rent, travel, and allied expenses. The plan indicated that any other special programs undertaken by the institute would be outside the operating budget, and thus needed to be separately financed. The annual operating budget was kept at the modest level of around $65,000. In order to undertake any real effort to raise resources we needed a board of trustees. In making the transition from CIC to Africa Service Institute (ASI) there needed to be an independent board. The founding members included Rawson L. Wood, a New York Catholic philanthropist and business leader; John Mosler, another philanthropist and business leader; Judge Samuel Pearce, who later in the administration of President Reagan would serve as secretary of Housing and Urban Development; and Monsignor Richard H. J. Hanley, publisher of the *Long Island Catholic*. Others would join an expanded board a year later. The president of the Institute was also designated as a board member. This established me both as the chief executive and as a trustee of the institute.

In looking for resources, the institute was fortunate in obtaining a subcontract from the Institute of International Education that would cover the costs of the student operation: assisting African students to find summer employment. We were fortunate that the climate for fundraising was favorable, especially in regard to the newly independent countries of the third world.

The late 1950s and early 1960s represented a weak point in the U.S. outreach to the third world countries. Former colonial powers, especially Great Britain and France, had long established government and private institutions ready to respond to the fast-moving events in Africa and other parts of the third world. This era was also the height of the Cold War and the Soviet Union was actively looking to become involved in the emerging nations. For the United States to catch up, both private and government resources had to be expanded. Africa Service Institute was part of this effort.

During this time I was still on the full-time payroll of John Price Jones and fortunately there was enough work, in addition to the CIC contract, to keep me employed. I felt that one of the important things that we could do was to be helpful to the African leaders when they visited the United Nations. I wanted to have a chance to discuss this concept with the leaders and was able to obtain a leave of absence with pay from Charles Anger, the chairman of the board of John Price Jones. This allowed me, in January 1960, to visit Senegal, Mali, Guinea, Ivory Coast, Ghana, Tanganyika, and Kenya. I did not visit Ethiopia because I had lived there for over a year and felt I knew the country well. I paid for the expenses of the trip to Africa from my personal funds.

It was this winter 1960 trip that energized me to develop my thoughts on how the American people could establish meaningful relationships with the African leaders. I was impressed on my visit with the leadership qualities of Haile Selassie, Tom Mboya, Julius Nyerere, Léopold Sédar Senghor, Sékou Touré, William V. S. Tubman, Felix Houphouet-Boigny, and Kwame Nkrumah. I returned home with determination to see that this should be an important part of the institute's activities. I was so enthusiastic about the quality of the African leaders that I had just met on the African trip that I decided to write a book. They were men with human weaknesses, but this group of leaders at the historical period of the 1960s in Africa was extraordinary.

I circulated my plan for a book on African leaders. Several publishers responded with interest and the Macmillan Company offered me a contract. While I was waiting for a solution to the funding problem of Africa Service Institute, I devoted full time to writing the book. The publisher wanted the manuscript as soon as it was possible for me to write it. It became my priority project and I submitted the manuscript in the early fall of 1960.

Published in 1961, *Profiles of African Leaders* was an immediate success. The *New York Times Book Review* gave it major coverage, and the same with other newspapers and journals known particularly in foreign affairs. Both the extensive media coverage of the book and the fast moving developments in

Africa in 1960 led to many speaking opportunities. It was my work with African students and eventually my book that were responsible for my introduction to Margaret.

In the fall of 1960, Margaret and her classmates at the College of New Rochelle had developed an interest in Africa and were often in New York at the African student events. I was introduced to this group of enthusiastic women by students from Tanganyika and Uganda. On March 7, formerly the Feast of St. Thomas Aquinas, Margaret, in her role as senior class president and knowing of my recent book, called me to invite me to speak at a conference on the Peace Corps being held the next week at the College of New Rochelle. I accepted.

When I arrived on campus, Margaret gave me a quick tour of the campus and took me to the auditorium. Following the questions that followed my talk, I gave an autographed copy of my book to Margaret J. Badum. On the following day, I phoned her and asked her to join me for dinner in New York. During one of our first dates, we went to a play on race relations. In the next few months, Margaret was coming to New York at least once a week and each time, because of strict residency rules, she asked for permission to leave campus because she was working on a project regarding Africa with Dr. Melady. On June 9, which was the day of her graduation and also her birthday, we became engaged.

The chairman of John Price Jones, where I was still employed, and Rawson Wood, who was chairman of the board of ASI, encouraged me to make a more specific visit to black Africa for the summer. Being just engaged, I hesitated to leave my fiancée for almost three months. Furthermore, it was going to be a busy summer at the institute. Margaret took a summer job at the institute and I left for Africa. There was no telephone contact; we did it all by letters. Margaret, who had already developed many African student friends, focused on helping arriving African students to find housing and employment. I returned with more enthusiasm than ever about the necessity to implement the plan that would simultaneously assist African students to find employment, to have funds available to assist with financial crises, and to assure that the African leaders, when visiting the United States, would not encounter annoying manifestations of racial prejudice in the areas of housing and employment.

When I returned in September there were still two challenges facing me: assuring the budget of ASI and completing the plans for our marriage. We needed around $25,000 to give us the needed $65,000 so the basic annual administrative budget was guaranteed. The Institute of International Education had approached us about subcontracting their work with African students and, especially, in identifying employment opportunities for them (on a part-time basis and during the summer vacation). They were also interested in assistance for identifying housing arrangements. This was especially challenging because at this time the Supreme Court and the Congress had not resolved the problem of racial discrimination in regard to housing. We also learned that some very limited government funds would be available in our work with African leaders. Since we were a 501(c)3 we planned to have several fundraising efforts. We found the fundraising came naturally to us, and we were quite successful at it. Overnight, over twenty countries in black

Africa were becoming independent, and there was no overall American strategy on how to meet this unusual political phenomenon; twenty independent states in one year. When African leaders came to visit the United Nations we could normally find citizens who would host a reception in their honor. These receptions were normally held in the homes of prominent New York City citizens.

Once the funding was assured I began to plan my own personal life. In 1961 I received an academic appointment at St. John's University in Long Island and began teaching a graduate course on U.S. foreign policy in black Africa. I had a similar arrangement with Fordham University. I also signed up with literary and speaking agents. I was pleasantly surprised, as it was the early 1960s, and these speaking engagements were more lucrative than I expected. I was also encouraged; I received contracts for a second and third book, *White Man's Future Black in Africa* and *Faces of Africa*. Macmillan was to be the publisher of *Faces of Africa*, which would include a chapter on each country. It was intended to be an auxiliary textbook.

It was an exceptionally busy fall as I worked on two books, gave speeches, taught at the university, and also prepared for our wedding on December 2. While I had actively sought both contracts for books and speaking engagements, the burden for planning the marriage fell on Margaret and her parents, who were very helpful with all of the details. I knew that it would be a very important day in my life. We were married at St. Gregory the Great Catholic Church in Bellerose, Long Island. African students were in the congregation and also the wedding party. During our honeymoon, Margaret and I, without any great responsibility believed that there was sufficient financial stability to begin our married life in New York City. When we returned Margaret immediately went to work on her master's degree.

We also spent some time discussing our dream that we could marshal the private sector, which included church-sponsored organizations, nonprofit groups, business and labor organizations, and others, so that we could influence African leaders who after decades of struggle had obtained their independence and would be choosing what type of governance they would recommend to their people.

Returning from the Caribbean we moved into what was my bachelor apartment on Nineteenth Street near Gramercy Park and began life together. We both strongly felt that an American-style democracy was preferable to Soviet Communism. In this book, we briefly sketched what we did in the period from 1960 to 1967. Were we successful in putting together this team? Did we have some influence so that the African people would not have to suffer the horrors of Communist rule?

In the following chapters we discuss the various African leaders that we met and maintained contact with from 1961 to 1968. Several became good friends, and we never lost touch with them over the years as our careers took us to new positions. It was a critical time in world affairs, as independence brought an end to old colonial structures and new personalities appeared on the scene. We had the privilege of being with them on numerous occasions. We relate not only the facts of our relationships, but also our opinion on how these leaders' political careers shaped, influenced, and affected the sweep of independence throughout black Africa.

Chapter One

LÉOPOLD SÉDAR SENGHOR

Poet, Philosopher, and Founding President of Senegal

On August 18, 1960, Tom met with Léopold Sédar Senghor — poet, philosopher, and African leader — in his office as president of the Federal Assembly of the Mali Federation. Tom was completing a summer visit to black Africa, finishing work on his book about African leaders. Little was known then about Senghor. He wrote all of his literary works in French. In an era when many African writers were calling for revolution, he talked about dialogue, universalism, and a convergence of cultures. He was a founder of the philosophy of "negritude," a collection of values that advocated close ties to France and the West in general.

Senghor had allocated only an hour for the meeting. The conversation turned from interesting to passionate when Tom introduced the name of Teilhard de Chardin into the conversation. Senghor immediately told him that he met Teilhard, the Jesuit priest-philosopher, when he was a university student in Paris and that Teilhard had saved him from falling victim to Marxism. Senghor invited Tom to return the next day so the conversation could be continued.

Back in his hotel room at the Croix du Sud, Tom reread some of the chapters from Teilhard's writings. At this second meeting, on August 19, 1960, Senghor was enthusiastic in his discussion of Teilhard de Chardin's ideas. He told Tom that he was delighted to find an American interested in the ideas of Teilhard de Chardin. He believed that the growing interdependence in the world and mankind's movement toward a universal civilization were reasons for optimism. Tom responded positively to Senghor's ideas and decided then that there would be a chapter on Senghor in his first book on African leaders, which was published in 1961.

When he was about to leave, Tom mentioned to Senghor that the next day he would visit Bamako, the other major city in the Mali Federation and the capital of the Sudan, Senegal's partner in the federation.

Senghor looked at Tom and in a quiet and serious tone said that there were problems in the federation and that it would be "better" for him to remain in Dakar for the next few days. Tom followed Senghor's advice. On the following day, August 20, the Mali Federation came to a bloodless end, and Senegal declared independence as a sovereign state. A few weeks later Senghor was declared president of the Republic of Senegal.

The breakup of the federation and the birth of a new African state occurred without any violence. Recognizing the obvious changes that were taking place in Africa, Senghor had always emphasized evolutionary movement that would avoid rupture and violence. Some political observers felt that he was an idealist dreamer and did not take his writings seriously. He had a very small following in the United States among Africanists.

When Tom departed Senegal, he returned to the United States via Paris as he wanted to talk with the Fathers of the Holy Spirit, who had provided the first schooling for Léopold Senghor. This group, primarily missionary priests, also founded Duquesne University, where Tom did his undergraduate studies. The priest who knew Léopold told Tom that as a young adolescent student he was already a rising star. At eight years old he began his education at the boarding school in Ngasobil, Senegal. The priest told Tom about Senghor's passion for languages and mathematics. He was a student for several years at their seminary but transferred to a secular school in Dakar when he recognized that he did not have a calling for a religious vocation.

His top academic grades in Dakar resulted in his being awarded a scholarship for higher studies in France. Senghor never forgot the early assistance that he received from the French missionary priests in Senegal. Later, as a University student and young professor in Paris, he was to meet a Jesuit priest, Pierre Teilhard de Chardin, who would guide him away from Marxism to become an intellectually strong Catholic layman.

Sweep of Independence

Tom's first meeting with Senghor took place at the beginning of the change that was to transform black Africa from a land of colonies to sovereign states. During his twenty years of active political leadership, 1960–80, Senghor served as the voice of orderly transition. Senegal was one of the few countries in Africa where political change was without any serious violence. A coup d'état has never taken place in Senegal since its independence.

As the natural urge for change grew in Africa, the fear that violence would serve as the means for achieving this goal for independence increased. It was always difficult to obtain recognition of Senghor's philosophy for evolutionary change based upon mutual respect for both Western civilizations and African culture.

We looked for ways to bring more attention to the viewpoints of Senghor. Fordham University accepted our suggestion to invite Senghor to give a major address on his belief in universal civilization and racial harmony. The university authorized a full academic convocation and awarded him an honorary doctorate of laws degree on November 2, 1961. At that ceremony, Senghor held the attention of the academic community with his analysis of the sweep of change taking place. He said,

> Man is saved since his hope has been maintained. We are now, all of us of different features, colors, languages, customs, stirred by the same movement of life. We are on the way towards the world of tomorrow, the world of the civilization of the universal.

After the convocation, we realized that he had spoken at too high an intellectual level for some who were more concerned about the "nuts and bolts" of independence. On the other hand, this was the persona of Senghor, a cultural intellectual dedicated to finding a harmonious solution to the racial, religious, and political tensions in Africa. We also regretted that some people who had been invited to the ceremony had declined to attend because they believed that Senghor was a French protégé who advocated positions that were unrealistic.

One of the guests who did attend contacted Tom several days later and complained about Senghor's philosophy of convergence when he said at the Fordham speech, "It is true also that Europe has destroyed in our countries many values of consideration, but it was in order to bring us other values into complements of our own values, meaning that we have stamped them with the seal of Black Africa." On the other hand, like Senghor, we both believed that positive evolutionary progress is an inherent part of Christian optimism. In his decades of active political leadership, Senghor continued to advocate the high moral road of evolutionary change and the acceptance of the forward movement to a merger of all civilizations that would result in what he termed "a civilization of the universal."

Senghor did not avoid applying his principles to complicated political situations. On June 4, 1978, after the public ceremony for Senghor at Sacred Heart University, where Tom served as president, the Meladys invited Senghor to a private dinner at the Fairfield Country Club. A number of political and diplomatic friends were present, including John Lodge, former governor of Connecticut and former ambassador to Spain and Argentina. Senghor gave an evaluation of the tensions generated by Fidel Castro in Africa. He called for discussions with the Cuban leader that would seek a peaceful solution to the tensions between the United States and Cuba, while showing respect for Cuban culture. In the course of the evening dinner, it was clear when the subject of Castro came up in conversation that Léopold Senghor was not comfortable with Castro's advocacy of revolutionary tactics. Tom transmitted a summary

Archives of Sacred Heart University

President Léopold Senghor being escorted by Thomas and Margaret Melady after receiving an honorary degree in 1978 from Sacred Heart University.

of these remarks to the White House staff for the upcoming meeting between Senghor and President Johnson.

Two years later in 1980, Senghor resigned from the Senegalese presidency. At this time he retired from public life. Abdou Diouf succeeded him in an orderly transfer. During the remaining twenty years before his death in December 2001, he continued to write poetry and to publish philosophical articles. He never stopped advocating nonviolent solutions to world tensions.

Early Years

The man who became the leading intellectual in Africa in the twentieth century was born in 1906 in a small village not far from Dakar. His father was a farmer, and Léopold was a product of a mixed marriage. His mother was a Christian and Léopold was baptized Catholic. Within a few years at the missionary schools, his teachers recognized that they had a brilliant young man. The missionary clergy arranged for him to complete his education in Dakar.

Léopold was treated like a "golden boy" and was awarded a scholarship for university studies in France. He majored in languages and literary studies. He soon became the "first African" to receive high French academic honors. He was the first black African to be appointed professor of the Lycée in France.

In Paris, Senghor became acquainted with a group of French-speaking intellectuals from the French colonies in the Caribbean — Martinique and French Guyana. Through literary works such as poetry, drama, and the novel, these young writers sought to wean their black readers from white culture, giving them an appreciation for their African heritage. They saw the connection between the cultural colonialism that inevitably estranged black populations from their heritage and the political colonialism that held large populations of black people in second-class status. Some, such as Frantz Fanon, a psychiatrist and philosopher from Martinique who later became a strong critic of Senghor, believed that cultural change would require political change and political change would happen only through violent revolution. Fanon mocked Senghor for his interest in the cultural framework of negritude and advocated that only through struggle would black Africa succeed. Inevitably, these revolutionaries were attracted to the communist ideology of popular resistance.

From the Caribbean intellectuals Senghor learned about the long and painful road of slavery and their desire to recapture a consciousness of their origins. Senghor began to see this concept of negritude as a possible philosophical basis for modern African nationalism. He told us that he had been attracted to these revolutionary ideas, but that he had resisted the urge toward violent upheaval. Then when he had been exposed to the writings and ideas of the French Jesuit philosopher Pierre Teilhard de Chardin, he began to see an alternative to revolution. After all, unlike his friends from Martinique and the Antilles, Senghor always saw harmony between his past life in the Senegalese village and his present life in Paris. As he grew in intellectual and political leadership, he advocated the position of evolutionary change: African people should have their own political independence while cooperating with the former metropolitan powers.

Prisoner of War

One little known fact in the history of Senghor was that after living in France from 1928 to 1932, he became a citizen of France. He freely accepted the responsibilities of citizen and accepted service in the French army. When war broke out between France and Germany, some French-speaking black intellectuals from the West Indies urged Africans not to partake in this conflict, but to concentrate their efforts on the fate of their own countries in Africa. Senghor did not follow this advice. As a French soldier he was captured and spent eighteen months in a prisoner of war camp. As would be expected, he not only learned German but also studied German culture.

It was there that some observers believe that he developed his concept that Africans are more intuitive and Europeans are more analytical. As he evolved in reputation and won many accolades, he maintained that philosophical position. He was criticized for oversimplifying the African persona as expressed in negritude.

Difficulties in Communication

We greatly admired the core of Senghor's philosophy: the formal movement of varying cultures to a universal civilization that would embrace all members of the human family. But it was difficult to obtain coverage of his philosophy in the national journals. One reason was the language problem. Though he wrote profusely, his writings were all in French. At this time, translations were slow in the making, and when translated, his thoughts, deeply rooted in classical thought, were difficult to explain. During the 1960s, a gloom existed regarding the prospects of racial harmony, and this continued to cloud the observations of many who dismissed Senghor as too optimistic and a "dreamer."

When we learned that President Senghor would visit the United States in the fall of 1963, Tom approached the John LaFarge Institute to sponsor a meeting with American religious leaders of all faiths. Father LaFarge was an early leader in the struggle for racial and social justice. On a beautiful October day, Senghor gave an analysis of why all Christian and Jewish leaders should *construire la Terre,* a reference to Teilhard de Chardin. His optimism was a source of inspiration to many of the leaders, who were facing growing tensions in U.S. society. There was a moving moment when at the reception all those attending joined Tom in a toast to a "noble man."

During the same visit, Senghor told the U.S. government official handling the details of his visit to New York City that he wished to visit the grave of Teilhard de Chardin. Tom was contacted and found out from the New York Province of the Jesuits that Teilhard was buried at the Jesuit cemetery in Hyde Park, New York.

President Senghor invited Tom to go with him in the official car that departed the Waldorf Astoria Hotel with a police escort. The entourage went directly to the cemetery at St. Andrews on Hudson, formerly a Jesuit novitiate, where President Senghor was greeted and escorted to Teilhard's burial site. An assistant gave him one rose, and kneeling in prayer he placed the rose next to the modest tombstone, which indicated Teilhard's date of birth, entry into the Society of Jesus, ordination, and death. Senghor evidently had noticed a member of the entourage filming his placing of the rose. His face flushed with anger, and he told the photographer to expose the film.

It was evident that Senghor wanted his moment with Teilhard to remain private and personal.

Disliked by Radicals

Tom's correspondence with Senghor grew. He invited Tom to visit him while he traveled to Canada. Tom flew to Ottawa on September 19, 1966. The next morning he went to the residence of the governor general for a 9:00 a.m. appointment.

When he arrived for his meeting with Senghor, the Montreal police were apprehensive. Tom's passport and identification were not sufficient to allow him to proceed to the suite of Senghor. Tom later learned that the police were looking for a man of his size, color, and appearance. The unidentified man carried a gun and made a determined effort to see Senghor.

After about twenty minutes Senghor emerged and embraced Tom. They both went up to Senghor's suite, where a lively conversation followed. Senghor remained passionate in his support for a committed dialogue to work out the racial and religious differences in Africa.

On several occasions Senghor indicated to us that he wanted to bring world leaders in the arts to Dakar to celebrate the contributions of African artists. Being a world traveler, he realized that there was only minimal appreciation in Europe and in the United States for art of the third world. He succeeded in 1966 in organizing the Third World Festival of Negro Arts in Dakar. Tom attended the festival but Margaret remained in Washington as we were expecting our first child, Christina. While many distinguished artists were there, including Duke Ellington and Langston Hughes from the United States, the European and American media coverage was not significant.

When Tom met privately with Senghor while he was in Dakar for the festival, he indicated to Senghor that his plans were to return full time to a university position. Senghor took advantage of this information to urge Tom to write more and promote more interest in the philosophy of negritude.

A year later in Dakar on November 22, 1967, an assassination attempt on Senghor's life occurred. Senghor survived, and in a note to Tom he reaffirmed his determination to continue his efforts for nonviolent change in Africa. Senghor's deep revulsion toward the use of violence to bring about change was the fundamental basis for his opposition to Soviet-supported Marxist alternatives that advocated revolutionary change. Senghor always had a strong commitment to evolutionary change, which was one reason for his fascination with the philosophy of Teilhard de Chardin.

After Tom completed his responsibilities at the Africa Service Institute in 1968, he was involved full time in his academic career. Our contacts with Senghor became less frequent. However, Embassy of Senegal officials in Washington invited us to some of their functions and remained in contact with us. Soon after Tom assumed the presidency of Sacred Heart University in 1976, he corresponded with Senghor about a visit to the university where he could address the university community.

In the spring of 1978, Senghor's staff informed Tom that he would be making an official visit to President Johnson in Washington, D.C., in early June. A convenient date for both the university and Senghor was identified, and on June 4, 1978, Senghor flew by helicopter to the campus, where a small but enthusiastic audience of faculty, students, and guests welcomed him. He gave a passionate address about man's movement for positive change. Senghor spoke in French and Margaret translated into English. We made a special effort to attract influential African Americans to the campus for the convocation. Senghor's commitments to nonviolent change and to negritude were still not known by many African American leaders in the 1970s.

Speaking about Castro, Senghor clearly raised questions about the alienation between many of the Cuban-Spanish community and the Afro-Cuban peoples, as well as Castro's commitment to Communism, which for Senghor was not a natural part of third world values.

In his private discussion with Tom before receiving the honorary degree, President Senghor indicated to Tom that his time as a public figure was coming to an end. He spoke passionately about his commitment to the central theme of Teilhard de Chardin's forward movement of the human family to a universal civilization. He clearly remained faithful to this belief that humankind was moving forward to a society free of many of the alienations of the past. He pointed out that in his own beloved country of Senegal there is an example of the change. Near his presidential residence in Dakar he would view Goree, the island that temporarily housed slaves before they were transported to North America or Brazil.

He once told us that his Catholic faith was part of the reason for his optimism about the future of the human family. He also told Tom that he looked forward to his retirement, as he would devote all his energies to writing about humankind's forward movement.

Senghor contributed directly to the intellectual growth of movements and philosophies that sought nonviolent solutions to the complex racial-religious and class differences that continued to grow. Now, five decades later after his active political leadership, there is a growing recognition of the merits of his passion for humanity's forward movement to a universal civilization.

The eloquent address that he gave on November 2, 1961, at Fordham University set forth a belief that humankind was on its way toward the world of tomorrow, "the world of civilization of the universal." This address, included here as Appendix 2 (see page 174 below), inspired us in our original efforts to communicate his optimistic vision of humankind to a larger audience. It was difficult to accomplish this because a significant number of those favoring independence for the African peoples felt his views were not practical. On the political level his advocacy of evolutionary change and universal pluralism also had its critics.

When his term as president came to an end, he retired to Normandy, France. Contrary to the trend among some African leaders, he indicated no interest in remaining in office "for life."

He became a member of the prestigious French Academy and continued his contacts with the worldwide intellectual community. On December 20, 2001 at the age of ninety-five, he died in France with his French wife and family at his side.

We were not able to be in France to attend the funeral. In the more than four decades since Tom first met Senghor in Dakar he was always faithful to his basic belief in humankind's destiny to move forward to a civilization free of the horrors of racial and religious prejudices. This was reflected in his writings. While they did not please those advocates who in the 1960s wanted immediate and revolutionary change, he remains a clear symbol of an important set of philosophical values expressed in his poetry and his writings.

Books by and about Léopold Sédar Senghor

Senghor, Léopold Sédar. *On African Socialism.* Introduced and translated by Mercer Cook. New York, Praeger, 1964.

———. *Prose and Poetry.* Translated by John O. Reed and Clive Wake. London: Oxford University Press, 1965.

———. *Selected Poems.* Introduced and translated by John Reed and Clive Wake. Oxford: Oxford University Press, 1964.

Guibert, Armand, and Seghers Nimrod. 2006. *Léopold Sédar Senghor: une étude.* Paris: Seghers, 1969 (1961 edition by Armand Guibert).

Hymans, Jacques L. *Léopold Sédar Senghor: An Intellectual Biography.* Edinburgh: Edinburgh University Press, 1971.

Markovitz, Irving Leonard. *Léopold Sédar Senghor and the Politics of Negritude.* New York: Atheneum, 1969.

Melady, Margaret. *Léopold Sédar Senghor: Rhythm and Reconciliation.* South Orange, N.J.: Seton Hall University Press, 1970.

Roche, Christian. *Léopold Sédar Senghor, le président humaniste*. Toulouse: Editions Privat, 2006. Preface by Abdou Diouf, *http://en.wikipedia .org/wiki/Abdou_Diouf.*

Spleth, Janice. *Léopold Sédar Senghor*. Boston: Twyane Publishers, 1985.

Vaillant, Janet G. *Black, French, and African: A Life of Léopold Sédar Senghor*. Cambridge, Mass.: Harvard University Press, 1990.

Chapter Two

JULIUS KAMBARAGE NYERERE
Patient Architect of Tanzania

When Tom was preparing for his visit to Africa in 1960 to obtain direct interviews with African leaders, he contacted the Spiritan Fathers at Duquesne University for the contact points of a young man who was a teacher at a school operated by these American Catholic missionaries in Africa. The Spiritan Fathers were specific in declaring that this man — Julius Nyerere — could discuss with Tom the aspirations of the African people. Father Francis M. Philbin, who had spent six years in East African mission work, was the Duquesne University staff member who assisted Tom for this visit.

In many ways the early years of Nyerere were similar to those of Senegal's Léopold Senghor. They were thousands of miles apart but were both identified by missionary priests as young men with solid leadership potential. Nyerere and Senghor were both encouraged to advance themselves through education.

Born on the eastern shore of Lake Victoria in 1922, Julius K. Nyerere was the son of a local tribal chief. A quiet and cooperative student, he attended local schools and then Makerere College in Uganda, where in 1946 he received a teaching diploma.

Again, like Senghor in Senegal, his talents were recognized by the European government administration. Tanganyika was then a United Nations Trust Territory administered by Great Britain, which facilitated Nyerere's acceptance at the University of Edinburgh in Scotland. He was the first Tanganyikan to study at a British university. When he returned to Tanganyika in 1952 with a master's degree, he arrived with considerable prestige.

It is believed that while at Edinburgh he began to develop his concept of socialism and self-reliance. It would later be defined as *ujamaa,* or familyhood, which would be a central point of the values he would advocate for the Tanganyikan people. The American missionaries who urged Tom to see him called him "man of the future."

Julius Nyerere's Teaching Career

As soon as he returned to Dar es Salaam, Nyerere received an assignment to teach history, English, and Kiswahili at St. Francis College on the outskirts of the city, but his teaching career did not last long.

Juluis Nyerere's career was evolving quickly. As Tom prepared for his January 1960 visit to Africa to interview the new leaders for his book, Nyerere was moving from teaching to the political arena. British administrators informed Nyerere that when he was elected president of the Tanganyika African National Union (TANU) he would have to leave teaching since TANU was a political organization. As Tom looked for Nyerere at St. Francis College in January 1960, Tom discovered that he was already in the city heading up TANU, the local African governmental organization.

The two days that Tom spent in Dar es Salaam looking in vain for Nyerere made him determined to arrange a future meeting as soon as possible. People spoke to Tom about Nyerere with awe and respect. He was told by several of Nyerere's aides at the hotel bar that there were two women who were very important to him. They were Joan E. Wicken, his personal assistant, and Lady Marion Chesham, an American-born widow of a member of the British House of Lords who had become a citizen of Tanganyika and a member of the Tanganyikan Parliament.

During the 1960s we were to hear the names of these two women frequently in Tanganyikan affairs. In the idle world of gossip, some tried to turn the trustworthy relationship of Nyerere with Joan Wicken into a secret romance. As a matter of practice, we deliberately refrained from participating in that type of gossip. Our own long experience with Nyerere left us with the belief that he was dedicated both to his country and his family.

In the 1960s world of African affairs, when there was a close relationship between the leader and a person not a citizen of the leader's country, the assumption frequently made was that the person was cooperating with one of the major intelligence agencies. In the case of Lady Chesham, the assumption was that she was connected to the British MI-6. We worked with Marion Chesham, who was a close confidant of Nyerere. We never asked her anything about the MI-6 rumor. In the 1960s and 1970s we learned to live in the developing U.S.-African gossip world where questions were asked, "Who is he or she actually working for?"

Nyerere carefully studied the approach that he would take in obtaining independence for his people. In 1955, as head of TANU he went to the United Nations and appeared before the committees responsible for the U.N. Trust Territories. Nyerere's appearance marked the first time that an African leader had been sent by a territorial political organization to present his people's views.

Tom understood enough about Nyerere and his country to write a chapter in his book *Profiles of African Leaders.* He gave the title of the chapter on Nyerere as "Architect of a New Nation."

Honorary Doctorate — Duquesne University

Between the time of Tom's missed appointment in Dar es Salaam due to the mixup of his address and Nyerere's quick rise to leadership in Tanganyika, we looked for a way to excite the academic community with the arrival on the international scene of another original thinker. Nyerere, like Senghor, lectured and wrote frequently. He would send us copies of his speeches, which covered a vast array of subjects: nonviolent methods to obtain independence, race issues, corruption as an enemy of the people, the functions of leadership, a national ethic, socialism and communal life, education and self-reliance, adult education, and lifelong learning.

Tom knew that Nyerere's yearly travel program often included a visit to the United Nations. Nyerere obviously

President Julius K. Nyerere of Tanzania.

appreciated the value of having full United Nations support not only for the independence of his country, but also for his concepts of independence, self-reliance, and African socialism. Tom looked around for an academic institution that would confer a top award on the young leader from East Africa. Several university presidents said that they would consider awarding Nyerere a certificate, but Tom wanted the highest university recognition, so he went to his undergraduate alma mater.

Tom suggested to Father Henry McAnulty, the president of Duquesne University and a member of the Spiritan order, that the university offer Nyerere an honorary doctorate and award it at a time convenient for Nyerere. There was no difficulty in obtaining this arrangement, as the Spiritan Fathers were enthusiastic about the role of this man of the future, not only in Tanganyika but also in African affairs more widely. The university gave a very quick approval.

A month after Tom returned from his visit to Africa, Nyerere arrived in the United States. Tom met with him in New York City in mid-February 1960 before he left for Pittsburgh to receive the degree on February 19, 1960. Nyerere was appreciative of the honor being bestowed on him, but had not yet prepared his acceptance remarks. Tom urged him to speak to the broad central issues of the sweep of independence occurring in all parts of Africa and in other countries of the third world, which were replacing colonial flags with their own newly minted flags. These were a visible demonstration of their independence and freedom.

Tom met Nyerere the day Nyerere was scheduled to leave for Pittsburgh. Having breakfast with him at the modest hotel where Nyerere was staying, Tom was surprised to learn that he would make his first trip to Duquesne on a bus! Tom also noted in his conversation that Nyerere spoke about the ideas of Teilhard de Chardin. In this regard, he had core values similar to those of Senghor. They spent their early years in various parts of Africa under different colonial systems. Somehow, they were touched by the same religious faith and by the philosophy of a towering figure who was not part of the conventional Catholic value system.

On Friday, February 19, at 3:30 in the afternoon in a special academic convocation, Duquesne University conferred on Julius K. Nyerere the doctorate of laws degree. In a brief, crisp citation the University declared,

> Your political acumen, your broad vision and quiet determination, joined in a truly devoted charity, have given new hope to men, long weary of racial strife and unresolved national differences. Your many years as a student and as a teacher have enabled you to bring the wisdom of the scholar into the often emotionally overcharged political atmosphere of a rapidly advancing Africa, where your counsels of reasonableness and moderation have made possible today what yesterday seemed only the wildest speculation.

He was a quiet, unassuming guest of the Spiritan Fathers at Duquesne. Nyerere later told Tom that at Duquesne he felt like he was at home. He also told Tom that he received recognition and honors but treasured especially the first honorary doctorate, as it came from the Spiritan Fathers, who found him as a young man and engaged him with the challenge of leadership. Much later, Lady Chesham told Tom that Nyerere had learned that other institutions felt it was too early to give an honorary doctorate to him. He appreciated more than ever the action of Duquesne and the role of Tom in nominating him.

The Role of Lady Chesham

Nyerere told Tom about the private community development organization that Lady Chesham, a member of the Tanganyikan Parliament, had founded. He praised her work profusely and asked Tom to relate this to Margaret. When we both went to Tanganyika in 1962, we met Lady Chesham and began a long relationship with her efforts to aid the rural people of her country. In 1958, Lady Chesham was chosen by TANU to run for a parliamentary seat from her area in the central part of the country. While she maintained her seat as a member of parliament from this period of transition and many years after independence, Lady Chesham spent much of her time organizing ways to assist in the rural development of her adopted country.

She had set up the Tanganyika Community Development Trust Fund to help fund projects that would benefit the educational and economic status of women and children. She asked us to join the American committee that supported this trust fund. We both accepted, but Margaret took the lead in this activity and worked closely with Jane Bagley Lehman, the first chair of the Tanganyika committee in New York, who supported Lady Chesham's trust fund through her family foundation. After Jane Lehman stepped down and Dr. Mabel Ingalls took over as chair, the Tanganyika committee became part of the Community Development Foundation headed by Glen Leet, who also was closely allied with Save the Children.

Lady Chesham told Margaret that she wanted her eventually to take over the responsibilities in New York, but Margaret resisted as we were starting our family with the birth of our first child. Nevertheless, Margaret remained in close correspondence with Lady Chesham, who wrote candidly to us about her opinions and reflections on Africa and Tanzania. She called the Rhodesian problem a "nightmare" and claimed that "Julius [Nyerere] and Kenneth [Kaunda] have managed to restrain the wilder African leaders" but the British government was "hopeless, making every blunder possible." Margaret remembers when Lady Chesham was angry with a writer who claimed that she was a confidant of Nyerere. However, through references to Nyerere in her letters, we knew that she was his trusted friend. Sometimes we wondered if she was voicing his thoughts when she wrote to us. As a European member of Nyerere's party, she had witnessed and played a role in Nyerere's efforts to forge racial harmony when black Africans assumed leadership. In 1965, she wrote of her fears during the Rhodesian difficulties, "The whole of Africa is on the edge of a volcano and all we have worked for is in dreadful danger."

Important Meetings

Following the closing of the Africa Service Institute and Tom's appointment as ambassador to Burundi in 1969, Tom had an experience with Nyerere that revealed much about the man and his values. In August of 1970, the White House informed

Tom that he would be recalled for four months of duty with the U.S. Mission to the United Nations. We would all return together. Our daughters would stay with Margaret's parents in Bellerose, New York, and we moved into a suite at the San Carlos Hotel near both the U.S. Mission and the United Nations. The term at the United Nations coincided with the fall semester at Seton Hall University, where Margaret was able to complete her courses for her master's degree.

Several weeks after Tom reported for duty at the U.S. Mission as the senior advisor on African affairs, he was attending a meeting of the U.N. General Assembly. He was called back to the U.S. Mission by a staff member who said that Dr. Henry Kissinger, then assistant to the president, had phoned and was obviously upset and left an urgent message for Tom.

Evidently before Nyerere left Dar es Salaam for the U.N. meeting in mid-September 1970, Dr. Kissinger had been in contact with Nyerere and had arranged a meeting between President Nixon and President Nyerere. President Nyerere would be picked up by a U.S. Air Force plane, taken to Washington, and then returned to New York.

Both sides had accepted the date for a Wednesday morning in late September. The office of a European leader, who had a meeting scheduled for the following day, contacted Dr. Kissinger and circumstances made it important that the meeting be scheduled for Wednesday, the same day and hour as had been set aside for Dr. Nyerere.

The appointment was changed for the convenience of the European leader. Dr. Kissinger phoned President Nyerere, who had already arrived in New York for the U.N. meeting. He asked

President Nyerere to change the date to the following day. He indicated that the United States would make all of the travel arrangements.

President Nyerere, to the surprise and the disappointment of Dr. Kissinger, indicated that he could not do this as he had a previously arranged appointment to visit the Maryknoll sisters in Ossining, New York. The message left for me indicated that Dr. Kissinger was shocked that President Nyerere could not (or would not) change his schedule because of a conflicting appointment with a group of Catholic sisters.

The instructions for Tom were very clear. He should call upon President Nyerere in New York and indicate the regrets of the U.S. government that he could not change his appointment with the religious sisters. Tom and Margaret discussed how we would handle this matter. Tom made the appointment, and we both saw Nyerere two days later at his Waldorf Astoria suite.

During the first fifteen minutes we had a pleasant conversation among friends. Nyerere told us that he was pleased with the actions of the church in elevating African priests to the rank of cardinal. He was a friend of Cardinal Rugambwa and praised his administration as archbishop of Dar es Salaam and thus titular leader of the Catholic Church in East Africa.

Margaret then presented him with an autographed copy of our recently published *House Divided: Poverty, Race, Religion, and the Family of Man.* This stimulated him to discuss some of his own ideas on race and reconciliation.

Tom then switched the conversation from personal to official. As a U.S. ambassador he said, "Your Excellency, I am here on instructions from the Office of the President to express our regret that you cannot arrange your schedule in order to visit with the U.S. President." Nyerere responded with his quiet boyish smile and told us how important the American Maryknoll sisters were to one of his self-reliance projects in Dar es Salaam.

As the nation's capital increased in size, the number of women seeking employment to augment their family income also grew. The sisters had set up training programs that taught such skills as dress making, cleaning clothes, and housekeeping. This would give them employment opportunities and lessen the possibility of the women falling prey to prostitution. As we listened to Nyerere describe the project we could sense how important it was for him. He told us that for these reasons he felt obligated to keep his appointment with the Maryknoll sisters. In regard to a visit with the president of the United States, he said he would be in contact with the president through the U.S. ambassador and hoped that a visit could be arranged the next time he was in the United States.

We immediately understood why a call on the sisters was more important than a visit with the U.S. president. Tom phoned the White House assistant and conveyed as best he could the feelings of President Nyerere. We have since discussed the matter and believe that it was a moment that confirmed for us the core of essential values of this quiet, unassuming leader from East Africa.

Mwalimu

A year later when Tom was back in Bujumbura as the U.S. ambassador to Burundi, Lady Chesham contacted us and said that at a recent meeting with Nyerere he had brought up our names and said, knowing that we were in neighboring Burundi, he hoped we would "drop by" for a visit before we departed Burundi.

Ambassadors cannot visit another country without obtaining the clearance of the local U.S. ambassador. Tony Ross, the U.S. ambassador and a friend, quickly gave us the clearance and a year after we saw Nyerere in New York we were in Dar es Salaam as the guests of Lady Marion Chesham.

Although Margaret had left the U.S. committee of the Tanganyika Community Development Trust Fund, she was still interested in assisting in obtaining resources for the fund. Marion was then living full time in Dar es Salam, where she could spend much of her time on the fund's activities and projects. Despite these priorities, Marion discretely kept in touch with Tanzanian politics.

For example, Marion was generally pleased with the American Embassy and the leadership of Ambassador Ross. This was not true of his predecessors. In the case of the first U.S. ambassador, Marion carried on a campaign against him. We were never able to determine if this was a signal she was conveying on the part of Nyerere or, as sometimes rumored, because of her alleged British MI-6 connection.

The arrangement was that we would attend Mass at a small Catholic church with Marion. Julius would be there but we would not sit with him. When we arrived, a few minutes before the start of the Mass, we immediately saw the president with several security aides. They were not in the front pew but in the middle. We discretely sat in the last pew. All of us received communion. After Mass, we proceeded to the picturesque little restaurant where Marion Chesham arranged for us to meet President Nyerere.

It was a very friendly, low-key conversation. He talked about the responsibilities of citizenship. He also thanked us for attending the Mass, which was still said in Latin at the church. He told us that he loved the Latin Mass.

He praised the work of Lady Chesham and thanked us for our assistance to her. As the coffee hour came to a close he wished both of us happiness in our work in Burundi and said "you are always welcome in our country."

After returning to Bujumbura, we both wondered if there was a purpose to the invitation to attend a Mass in Latin with him and Lady Chesham and to have a coffee afterward. We always retained our affection for Marion because we remember how she helped us to prevent an embarrassing situation. On one occasion, she told us about the reservations that Nyerere had about the U.S. Peace Corps. Nyerere had told her that the young people in the Peace Corps were dedicated idealists, but he believed that Tanzania was not the right place for them because the Peace Corps stressed capitalism and competition, and these ideas conflicted with African values of socialism and accommodation. Fearing the probability of open conflict over the presence of the Peace Corps, Tom urged Marion to influence Nyerere to work with the U.S. Embassy and to orchestrate a gradual withdrawal.

The 1971 meeting in Dar es Salaam was the last time we saw Julius Nyerere and Lady Chesham. He would be the advocate of *ujamaa*, socialism, self-reliance, and education. His core principles always focused on development and the critical importance of the African peoples developing and implementing their own concepts based on their values.

The country went from Tanganyika to Tanzania when, in a cleverly arranged political operation, it absorbed Zanzibar. The country became a republic in 1962, and Nyerere was the first president. He was admired for leading the country through the political process of obtaining independence without violence and inspiring high standards for racial and religious reconciliation. However, political leaders in both Europe and the United States suspected his dialogue and cooperation with Russian and Chinese trade and economic aid missions. Our enthusiasm for Julius Nyerere was well known, and we sometimes were ridiculed for an "infatuation."

Ujamaa, the central doctrine of Nyerere rooted in his ideas of family socialism, was always difficult to explain. One reason was that in the Cold War atmosphere, some felt *ujamaa* was too close to communism. This fact combined with Nyerere's strong commitment to "nonalignment" made him vulnerable to rumors that he was not in any way pro-West, but in fact had basic philosophical sympathies with socialism. A Catholic intellectual, he studied the writings of Teilhard de Chardin but was able to retain the "common touch" with Tanzanians.

We recognized this and knew that one reason for our respect for him was that he was a deeply religious man. It was always apparent that his early study with the American Spiritan Fathers gave him the foundation that remained with him for all his life. He never questioned the early teachings of the church on the nature of a just society.

In 1985 he retired from public life. While his "bigger than life" persona was always present, he never interfered with the demo-cratic process in his country. In his later years he was frequently referred to as *Mwalimu* — the Teacher. Julius Kambarage Nyerere died in London on October 14, 1999. His funeral ceremony in Dar es Salaam on October 21 was attended by U.S. Secretary of State Madeleine Albright, who represented President Clinton and the American people. Tom was alone in Washington, D.C., on that day (while Margaret was in Rome serving as president of the American University in Rome) and participated in Mass at the Cathedral of St. Matthew. There were only a handful of people at the Cathedral in Washington who were aware of the passing of the quiet, unassuming architect of a new state in Africa.

Books by and about
Julius Kambarage Nyerere

Nyerere, Julius Kambarage. *Freedom and Development: Uhuru na Maen-deleo: A Selection from Writings and Speeches 1968–1973.* Oxford: Oxford University Press, 1973.

———. *Ujamaa: Essays on Socialism.* Oxford: Oxford University Press, 1968.

Legum, Colin, and G. R. V. Mmari, eds. *Mwalimu: The Influence of Nyerere.* London: Africa World Press, 1995.

Petruk, B. G., Institut Afriki. *Julius Nyerere: Humanist, Politician, Thinker.* Dar es Salaam, Tanzania: Mkuki na Nyota Publishers, 2005.

Chapter Three

KENNETH DAVID KAUNDA
Zambian Navigator for Freedom

Racial reconciliation was always a key interest for us. Southern Africa was thus a challenge in the 1960s. In preparing for his January 1960 trip to Africa and seeking interviews for his book on the emerging young leaders, Tom sought the counsel of Father John LaFarge, S.J., an activist for ending racial discrimination. He advised Tom to contact two Irish Jesuit priests residing in Lusaka, the then capital of Northern Rhodesia, now Zambia.

Within several hours of arriving in Lusaka, Tom was at the Jesuit residence and met with Father Patrick Walsh, S.J., and Father Robert Thompson, S.J. Tom was overwhelmed by the enthusiasm that he found with the two Irish priests for assisting the African majority in their desire for freedom and independence. Tom was impressed that even in the area where white racial superiority was openly preached, there was an oasis where freedom and independence were actively advocated. With clarity and determination, the two Irish missionaries immediately told Tom about a young African schoolteacher who could provide the leadership for the local African people. Furthermore, they told Tom, he believed in and was committed to racial reconciliation.

The Irish priests' candidate was Kenneth David Kaunda. Tom was surprised, as U.S. government friends had recommended that he meet Harry Nkumbula. In fact, one senior government official bluntly told Tom that Harry Nkumbula was the man who could lead the Northern Rhodesia Africans to independence. Tom had arranged an appointment to meet Nkumbula the following day.

For Tom, after he met both Nkumbula and Kaunda and engaged them in conversation, there was not any doubt who was the leader that, in the delicate situation of Northern Rhodesia, would provide effective and inspiring leadership. Tom expressed this candid opinion to the Department of State. Tom was especially impressed with Kaunda's strong commitment to racial reconciliation.

When Tom departed Lusaka in January 1960, the sweep of independence in all of black Africa was about to start. He realized that the success of the sweep would vary in all parts of Africa. In central and southern Africa, the transition would be affected by the local attitudes on race relations. The need in central Africa was for a leader who understood racial reconciliation. He believed that the Irish Jesuits made the right decision to assist Kaunda in his early political undertakings.

Early Life

Kaunda was born on April 28, 1924, in Chinsali Northern Rhodesia (now Zambia). His father, the Rev. David Kaunda, was an ordained Church of Scotland clergyman. Kenneth Kaunda always classified himself as a Presbyterian. The culture of an active Christian life permeated all aspects of the youth of Kaunda.

He was influenced by destiny, like the other African leaders of that period. In Kaunda's case, he was born and spent his youth in that part of Africa where the white minority was protected and favored by the colonial governments in the then Northern and Southern Rhodesia. These two countries were next-door neighbors to South Africa, which at that time proclaimed the cause of the white man's racial superiority.

It was the decade that preceded the sweep of independence that overtook most parts of black Africa in the 1960s. Kenneth Kaunda was able to sense that his country should be part of this dynamic change. He resented the racial discrimination that was being practiced in central Africa. He was one of the co-founders of the African National Congress (ANC), which almost immediately became the primary anticolonial organization in Northern Rhodesia. From 1953 to 1958, he served as secretary general and was the top deputy to Harry Nkumbula, the president of the ANC.

Kaunda, a practicing Presbyterian, easily formed alliances with those of other denominations. His close alliance with the Irish Jesuit missionaries was an example. He faced the blunt truth of the white-dominated Federation of Rhodesia and Nyasaland. Kaunda, in responding to this challenge, did not accept the inevitability of the use of violence. He completely rejected it as a means to obtain freedom and independence for his people. In the mid-1950s he visited India and practiced with enthusiasm the nonviolent principles of Gandhi. His commitment to nonviolence combined with a passionate practice of Christianity came at a time when the sun was setting on European colonialism. We always believed that Kaunda was influenced by the basic Christian values that he embraced starting with his youth.

We both said to friends in and out of U.S. government circles that Kaunda was an appealing authentic figure who could inspire both reconciliation and cooperation among the three racial communities in Northern Rhodesia; the black Africans (who were the overwhelming majority), the whites, and the Indians, who were very small minorities. He practiced engagement in the early days of his career.

We knew the history of Kaunda. When the Federation of Rhodesia and Nyasaland was created he fought against the color bar. He always avoided the temptation to use violence. The local white-dominated power structure in 1953 sent him to prison. After months of incarceration he was banished to the countryside.

The events in Northern Rhodesia moved very quickly; it was like "breaking news." We both believe that the leadership of one leader who has both the ability and stability to play such a role can influence the outcome of events. The ingredients in the Northern Rhodesia situation in the early 1960s were explosive. We agreed with our Jesuit friends in Lusaka that Kaunda had the qualities to be the quarterback of a serious political strategy.

Kaunda visited the United States on several occasions in 1961 and 1962. We saw him each time. Our estimation of his unique leadership qualities grew. We searched for the opportunity to obtain for him national recognition that would enhance his ability to give strength to his nonviolent campaign for freedom and independence.

In 1963 he was a party leader but had no official government leadership position. We told him about our plan to arrange an academic convocation where he would be awarded the honorary doctorate of laws degree. He told us that he could absent himself from the "breaking news" political tensions of Lusaka in April or May 1963.

With the strong support of the chairman of the board of Africa Service Institute, Rawson L. Wood, and senior trustees John Mosler and Samuel Pearce, we nominated him for an honorary doctorate at Fordham University. We pointed out to Father McGinley, S.J., then president of the university, that we knew that "a chance" was being taken on conferring the university's highest academic accolade on a political leader who had not yet received recognition from his own country. Fordham University had a long list of worldwide leaders who had received their honorary doctorate. In fact the country was not yet independent. Father McGinley said that he understood and gave Tom his approval to move ahead and arrange a date that was convenient for Kaunda.

High Honors: A Political Purpose

Tom contacted Kaunda, and he informed us that late May would be a convenient time. We also invited his wife, Betty, as we wanted to give an African leader the same respect and dignity as a leader from Europe. Kaunda had told us in a 1962 visit to correspond with him on sensitive matters through Father Walsh. He had evidence that his mail was being opened up by the Rhodesian intelligence services. This Irish Jesuit priest was to play a significant role in all our contacts with Kaunda, even after he became president of the republic.

The week of introducing Kenneth as the man who had the ability and dedication to lead Northern Rhodesia to independence without violence started in mid-May 1963. Tom had outlined the plan in a letter to Father Walsh on April 5, 1963. In the letter to Father Walsh Tom said,

> Dear Father Walsh,
>
> I am writing to you about the LL.D. degree which has been offered to Kenneth by Fordham University. I thought that it would be easier for me to point out these matters to you and that you might call them to the attention of Kenneth in your own way.
>
> 1. The offering of an LL.D. degree to a political leader who is not head of state or head of government is rare. Fordham University, who has awarded such degrees to Presidents Roosevelt, Eisenhower, and Kennedy, Chancellor Adenauer, Sir Winston Churchill, the prime minister of Ireland, President Senghor, and the late President Olympio, is taking special cognizance of what Mr. Kaunda *has already done for his people and the world.*

2. A special convocation will be held,

    a. which will be attended by U.N. Delegates.

    b. American academic leaders.

    c. here, Mr. Kaunda can give a major message. From this platform, he can give an address which, owing to the circumstances, will be covered by the world-wide press which will be invited to send their reporters to the ceremony.

3. Following the convocation a "black tie" (formal) dinner will be held:

    d. where Kenneth will meet and speak with around 35 leading private U.S. citizens. This affair will *not* be covered by the press and Mr. Kaunda can be quite frank in his remarks.

    e. it will give Kenneth an opportunity to meet personally those prominent people.

4. April and May are excellent months to do something like this. Is there any chance that Kenneth could come this month or in May? We would like about two weeks to get ready for it.

I know that you would have your own way of pointing these matters out to Kenneth. Please let me know what the results of your conversation are.

Under separate cover I am mailing you a catalog from Fordham University.

This was our plan to present Kaunda with appropriate dignity to the influentials of New York. Kaunda responded in a telegram saying he would be pleased to accept and suggested anything after mid-May 1963. "Glad to inform you that I accept the honor bestowed on me by board of trustees of Fordham University."

The event occurred as arranged on May 21, 1963. Father McGinley and his colleagues appreciated the significance of having an African leader leading a nonviolent campaign for independence as the recipient of their honorary doctorate. He consulted Tom about the citation. Tom urged that Kaunda be cited for the fight against racial discrimination. It was a special convocation, and Kaunda was the center of attention as he was the only degree recipient. He spoke movingly after the degree was conferred. African members of the diplomatic corps and civil rights representatives were there. The African diplomats immediately recognized the significance of the event. Kaunda had no governmental position; his country was not yet independent. Nonetheless, President Kennedy sent a telegram of congratulations to Kaunda acknowledging his role as a leader of the people of Zambia.

The Fordham University president concluded with these words in the Honorary Degree citation:

Through varying chances and so many hazards he now stands forth a leader of his people whose reputation has reached all parts of Africa and the whole world. Filled with deep admiration for these among his other merits, the University has resolved to confer upon such a distinguished lover of liberty and justice our highest mark of academic distinction.

Archives of Fordham University

President Kaunda being congratulated by Fordham University officials
Father McGinley and Father Vincent O'Keefe, in 1963.

The black tie party was especially successful. Kaunda met
a number of well-connected social leaders. While his acceptance remarks at the convocation ceremony were too long and
too detailed for an American audience, his gracious attitude at
the reception gave him time to socialize with a social elite. He
was recognized as a leader who could inspire a high level of
influential people to support his policies.

He and his wife, Betty, remained in the United States for
another week.

A few weeks after the convocation, the president of the university received a letter from a Jesuit missionary priest in Lusaka

(who was not a Irish Jesuit) protesting the award. He based his protest on the basis that Kaunda was not a "head of state." The convocation predicted what would happen. Kaunda became the first president of the Republic of Zambia on October 24, 1964, sixteen months after receiving the honorary doctorate, which was designed to put him in a position where he would be a strong candidate for the position.

Independence Ceremonies

We were both invited to participate in the independence ceremonies in October 1964. Tom was preoccupied with duties in New York. Margaret accepted, stopping first in Rome to attend the canonization ceremonies of the Ugandan saints. It was a historic moment for the Catholic Church and Africa. When Pope Paul VI, assisted by Tanganyikan Cardinal Rugambwa and Ugandan Archbishop Kiwanuka, decreed that the Ugandan martyrs had been inscribed in the catalog of saints, one heard twenty-two new and different sounding names — Musaka, Ngondwe, Kaggwa. Practically all those in attendance at the canonization were black Africans. Among the ranks of cardinals present, Margaret found faces of all races. African drums heralded the joyous news welcoming these saints into a new era for the Catholic Church.

Arriving in Lusaka, Zambia, Margaret immediately called on Father Walsh, who reported that Kenneth's trip to Ireland had been arranged, as well as a state visit to the Vatican. We had suggested these arrangements to Father Walsh on a previous visit. The next day, Margaret met John Mosler, a trustee of the

Africa Service Institute, who, with Mrs. Etta Barnett, had been appointed to the official U.S. delegation, headed by Charles Engelhard. The independence ceremonies attracted an array of diplomatic and business personalities. The Princess Royal represented the British Queen; Ralph Bunch the United Nations. Among the Americans were Arthur Houghton and Mr. and Mrs. Harry Oppenheimer, an indication of the significance of the Zambian transition and its influence on the remaining nations and territories in southern Africa.

Margaret's attendance at the ceremonies provided excellent opportunities to further the work of the Africa Service Institute. Together with John Mosler, she was able to further our relationships with Zambian and other African leaders present at the ceremonies. She introduced Angolan leader Holden Roberto to Father Walsh and others who were assisting refugees from the Portuguese territories.

There was only one negative aspect to the event: the head of the U.S. delegation. Margaret was questioned by every African she met as to why Charles Engelhard was appointed head of the delegation. Most voiced their strong disapproval. Engelhard's association with South African apartheid was paramount in their view. But Engelhard was also gruff, rude, and generally dismissive of black Africans. The Engelhards gave a reception prior to the evening's ball, but not one African was present, and in fact Margaret never saw them socially with any Africans during the entire period. When John Mosler suggested that they meet privately with some African leaders from areas seeking independence, Engelhard told John that he could not and would not meet with any revolutionary. Fortunately, delegation members

John Mosler and Etta Barnett, remaining apart from the Engel-hards as much as possible, met with African delegations and Zambians and thus helped to foster genuine relationships both officially and socially.

Ten years later, we received a letter from the director of Zam-bia's Tenth Anniversary Independence Celebrations, telling us that President and Mrs. Kaunda had nominated us as "their very best friends" to participate in the celebrations. Tom had just become executive vice president of St. Joseph's University and so Margaret once again represented the family. Much had changed. Government structures were more developed, the city had grown with new facilities. Some of the African leaders who had attended the independence ceremonies came to celebrate ten years later. Once again, Margaret had a chance to renew friendships.

Underlying Moral Questions

Kaunda always emphasized the underlying moral question when discussing world issues. In 1968 he invited us to join him in Uppsala, Sweden, on July 6, where he would address the Fourth Assembly of the World Council of Churches. Our second daugh-ter, Monica, had arrived prematurely a few months before, and we were not able to attend. He sent us a copy of the speech. His words represented a penetrating analysis of the problems of the developing world. The "poor-rich" divide still is a serious cause for concern in the world.

In the 1966–68 period, Kaunda was in regular contact with us. Tom recommended that he write in detail to Pope Paul VI about the dangers of racial clash in southern Africa. As the

health of the Portuguese leader declined, Tom urged Kaunda
to engage the Portuguese leadership over their problems in
Angola and Mozambique. Kaunda was the only African revolutionary leader of that time who was in contact with the
government of Portugal. The issue at hand was the increasing number of Mozambican and Angolan refugees coming into
Zambia. Kaunda's outreach to the leadership of Portugal for a
solution to the problems of Angola and Mozambique was part of
his commitment to finding nonviolent solutions. He practiced
engagement.

In August 1968 Kenneth informed Tom that he would be
in Paris in mid-September. Tom's work with the Africa Service
Institute was coming to an end, and he was making the transition to the life of a professor. But he remained curious about
what Kenneth was thinking after several years as president of
Zambia.

Since the United States was at the eve of a new administration, it would be President Humphrey or President Nixon. Tom
decided to go to Paris and met with Kaunda on September 18,
1968. Tom made the following memorandum on the meeting:

I, first of all, complimented Kenneth on the excellent
address that he gave at the opening session of the International Conference of Human Rights. He hit very hard
on the responsibility of the West to solve the South African
problems.

"It is a long time since we have seen each other," Ken
said, "and I want to confide in you my worries about the
United States." They were basically:

1. growing violence in the United States

2. turn to the political right

3. decline of interest on the part of the administration, in Africa

I discussed the three items at some length, and believe that he felt a little more relaxed about it. Ken seemed to have the idea that the election of Mr. Nixon would mean a dramatic turn to the right. I, first of all, tried to put Mr. Nixon into the correct setting — his background, philosophy, etc. I found that Ken responded quite warmly to my analysis and said that it was important for the United States to regain its sense of moral leadership in the world. [In regard to the emerging African leaders of the 1960s and their opinion of Richard Nixon, most of them felt like Kaunda. It would be a turn "to the right." The one exception to this view of Nixon was Tom Mboya.]

He asked me about visiting the United States. I said that, in any case, he should wait until after inauguration. I also advised him to avoid coming over informally, but this time to see an official head of state. He seemed quite pleased with the suggestion and said that we should continue corresponding on it.

I told Ken that I felt it was important for the Catholic Church to speak on human rights this year, and that a good part of the document should be devoted to racism. I asked him to write directly to Pope Paul, asking for such a document and he said that he would. I am writing to remind him of this. [Ken had told Tom how pleased he was with his 1966 audience with Pope Paul VI.]

Ken was going to the Ivory Coast to see Houphouet-Boigny and asked me to brief him on the Ivory Coast leader, which I did.

His wife, Betty Kaunda, was in Paris with him after a visit of some weeks in Germany.

Visit to Zambia

Soon after arriving in Burundi, where Tom took up his post as U.S. ambassador, Kenneth wrote a thoughtful and gracious letter inviting us to visit him and Betty. As in the case of visiting Julius Nyerere, Tom needed to consult with the U.S. ambassador to Zambia. He did, and Ambassador Oliver Troxel was positive about us visiting Lusaka and calling on President and Mrs. Kaunda. In fact, Ambassador Troxel invited us to stay with him for our three-day visit in May 1970.

We had a very good "updating" visit with Kenneth and Betty. It was still in the early period of independence, and he was still very determined to work with the various religious communities. He was a natural ecumenist. There were evidently some problems in finalizing an arrangement with the Catholic Relief Services and, as a result, the worldwide Lutheran Relief organization was invited to handle the refugee problem in Zambia. We later learned that it was primarily a matter of personalities.

In commenting on the differences, both of us in the brief three-day visit to Lusaka observed how active the newly established Embassy of China was. Our visit was during the height of the Cold War. Kaunda spoke to us of economic assistance from the East and the West, and we were then comforted by the feeling that Kaunda wanted to be "even handed."

During the 1970s our contacts were less frequent. It was during the height of the Cold War, and Kaunda had become a very strong supporter of the Non-Aligned Movement (NAM). After hosting a NAM summit in Lusaka in 1970, he served as its chairman from 1970 to 1973. Kaunda was a strong supporter of Marshal Tito, the long-time authoritarian leader of Yugoslavia who was also a strong pillar of strength in a Non-Alignment Movement. At the funeral ceremonies of Tito in 1980, Kaunda openly wept. Tom was asked if this indicated any kind of instability. Tom responded that personal loyalty had always been one of Kaunda's characteristics.

Last Years as President

When Tom returned to New York and reflected on his discussion with Kenneth in Paris on September 29, he wrote to Kenneth on two actions that he was promoting and wanted to influence Kenneth to do so.

Dear Ken,

It was good to see you and Betty again in Paris. It had been too long a time!

After seeing you, I went to Rome. I believe that it is now quite likely that the Holy Father will issue a significant document on human rights, and that a good part of it will be devoted to racism. I know that a letter from you would be very meaningful, and I would like to suggest the following:

1. Write to His Holiness about your concern over the continuing violation of human rights throughout the world.

2. Your special concern about southern Africa. Enclose a copy of the address that you delivered at the International Conference on Human Rights on September 16, 1968, in Paris.

As the framework for the new administration develops, I will send you brief items of interest.

It looks like there will be a new government in Portugal. Appreciating your commitment to dialogue whenever possible, I would like to suggest that you write to the new Prime Minister when he is appointed, renewing your offer to serve as an intermediary. We should really expect that no one in Lisbon will change, but, who knows — with a new Prime Minister. I would also like to suggest that you write to the newly elected president of the United States, shortly after the November election, congratulating him and then, urging him to use his good offices to suggest that the new Prime Minister of Portugal guide Portugal to review its policy in Africa and study what Spain did in Guinea — as this might give some ideas to Portugal on how to resolve their African problem.

We followed the career of Kaunda, who remained as president and chief of state until 1991. In our early contacts with him we appreciated his commitment to moral principles, but were concerned about how he expressed these commitments. We began to learn about incidents where there were questions about his presidential judgment while still serving as chief of state.

In April 1975 we learned that President and Mrs. Kaunda would be the guests of President Gerald Ford. They would be here on a "friendship visit." The two-day visit comprised a heavy schedule of appointments, including a meeting of President Kaunda with President Ford in the Oval Office.

The final part of the visit was a state dinner at the White House. Jean M. Wilkowski, a pioneer woman ambassador in the U.S. Foreign Service, was then the U.S. ambassador to Zambia. President Ford, the host, gave a generous introduction to President Kaunda, which included remarks like, "America knows and respects you; . . . we look to your wise counsel." The "black tie" guests, after hearing the words of appreciation, were suddenly surprised to hear Kaunda's sharp words of criticism. This was an official state dinner and President Kaunda was the guest of the U.S. president.

While President Ford's speech took about the normal twelve to fourteen minutes, Kaunda went on for around fifty minutes. At the height of his criticism he charged that "America has not filled our expectations in the struggle for independence . . . and building peace in Southern Africa." He, with a tone of bitterness, said that American policy "had given psychological comfort to the forces of evil."

In the course of his remarks he also gave the distinct impression of involving himself in the internal affairs of the United States. President Ford was a Republican and President Kaunda went on to praise an icon of the Democrat Party, G. Mennen Williams, who was assistant secretary for African Affairs in the Kennedy-Johnson years. The criticisms of the U.S. policy were very similar to the ones articulated to Tom by Kaunda at their meeting in Paris in September 1968.

We learned about the shock and surprise caused by the remarks of President Kaunda from career friends serving in the U.S. Department of State. Our singular defense of him was that he had strong moral convictions and that he preferred honest talk to diplomatic traditions. There is no question that he shocked the U.S. diplomatic community by confronting the U.S. president publicly with his views. Another reason for these departures from standard rules of protocol may have been because Kaunda was surrounded by an incompetent and perhaps inadequate staff. Competent and loyal assistants would have called these matters to his attention and could have, if he wished, found a better way and place to express these concerns.

His twenty-seven years as the founding president of Zambia were full of challenges. His decision to eliminate multiparty elections for one party rule will always be the subject of criticism by Western political analysts. Now in retirement, he praises the multiparty system of Zambia. However, when asked, he defends the one-party system in force during most of his twenty-seven-year reign. Given the struggle in southern Africa and the height of the Cold War, he believed that a multiparty system would have been used by external interests and would have been very harmful in those early years of an emerging state.

Kenneth David Kaunda is now retired. One of the few remaining African leaders of the 1960s still alive, he will ultimately be

evaluated by historians on his role, first for the Zambian people
and for then the people of the world.

Our experiences go back to the 1960s when he stood proudly
at the United Nations calling for nonviolent change from white
minority control and for the right of the African majority to
freedom and independence.

Political leadership in these circumstances requires daily judg-
ments. Some of his can be questioned, however, in totality we
believe that Kaunda warrants the citation given to him in an
honorary degree ceremony in 1963. He was a true navigator for
freedom.

Books by and about
Kenneth David Kaunda

Kaunda, Kenneth. *State of the Nation: Politics and Government.* Lusaka:
Kenneth Kaunda Foundation, 1988.

Kaunda, Kenneth D., and Colin M. Morris *The Riddle of Violence.* San
Francisco: Harper & Row, 1981.

Hall, Richard. *The High Price of Principles: Kaunda and the White South.*
New York: African Publishing Corp., 1969.

Macpherson, Fergus. *Kenneth Kaunda: The Times and the Man.* New
York: Oxford University Press, 1974.

Mulford, David C. *Zambia: The Politics of Independence, 1957–1964.*
London: Oxford University Press, 1967.

Ranganathan, M. A., and Kenneth David Kaunda. *The Political Philosophy of President Kenneth D. Kaunda of Zambia.* Lusuka: Kenneth
Kaunda Foundation, 1986.

Wilkowski, Jean M. *Abroad for Her Country: Tales of a Pioneer Woman
Ambassador in the Foreign Service,* chap. 10. Notre Dame, Ind.:
University of Notre Dame Press, 2008.

Chapter Four

SERETSE KHAMA

Courageous Advocate for
Racial Reconciliation in Botswana

A name that frequently came into discussion in the transition period between the Catholic Interracial Council and the formation of the Africa Service Institute was Seretse Khama of the then Bechuanaland. Seretse Khama, the son of African royalty, while a student in London fell in love with a young English woman, Ruth Williams, who was white.

The Seretse-Ruth Story

It was in the late 1950s and early 1960s, and race relations in both England and the United States were at a high point of tension. On the one hand, in the United States many African Americans were benefiting from the availability of higher education. Both the Catholic and Protestant churches and the Jewish synagogues were being pushed by their leadership to reduce the racism that still existed within their ranks and simultaneously to seek reconciliation.

These developments were related to the purposes of the Catholic Interracial Council of New York. Assisted by the

Archdiocese of New York, the Council fortunately had as its leader Rawson L. Wood, a New York business leader. He gave the council the leadership to identify ways to seek racial reconciliation. A prominent Jesuit activist, Father John LaFarge, was also a strong leader in this effort. Father LaFarge was also influential in the founding of the Africa Service Institute.

In 1960, Cardinal Francis Spellman, archbishop of New York, was concerned about the large number of African diplomats who were coming to New York City as a result of their countries being admitted as members of the United Nations. The sweep of independence in Africa was having an impact. How would these African visitors be treated when it came to housing and employment opportunities for their spouses and family? This was the situation, as previously pointed out, that inspired the CIC to establish a nonprofit organization that would focus on black Africa.

The Seretse-Ruth story was well known among interracial groups. As we met with African leaders in the early 1960s, we started our efforts to be in contact with Seretse, but it was not easy for various different reasons.

Seretse Khama was born into a privileged class. On the day of his birth, July 21, 1921, he was immediately recognized as heir to the local chieftaincy. His father died when he was four, and as a royal prince he was placed under the authority of his uncle, Tshekedi Khama. Young Seretse inherited the goodwill of the British government. He was the grandson of Khama III, who formed an alliance with the British government in the nineteenth century and thus allowed the British to consolidate their colonial authority in that part of southern Africa.

Seretse attended local schools that all operated within the apartheid system. He witnessed racial separation at a very young age. In 1944 he received a bachelor of arts degree from the University of Fort Hare. Anxious to move forward rapidly and financially supported by family and government funds, he immediately started his law studies at the University of Witwatersrand. He transferred the following year as he told his friends he knew that being in England would help his career. He enrolled at Oxford University.

Seretse enjoyed both his studies and life in London. In 1948 he completed his law studies and married Ruth Williams, the white woman he loved. An heir to a tribal chiefdom in the Bechuanaland, this black African created a sensation when the marriage took place in a civil court in London. The newspapers of England compared the Seretse-Ruth marriage to that of King Edward VIII, who abdicated the throne of England to marry the woman he loved, the American divorcee, Mrs. Simpson.

Preparing for Independence

Seretse Khama and Ruth Williams settled in London as a newly married couple. There was not much choice for them as the British government decided that British authorities would not recognize Seretse Khama's chief position for at least five years. Seretse focused on the future. He utilized this period to maintain and expand his contacts in Bechuanaland. He also cultivated additional friends in the British establishment.

He realized that once back in his country he would need to work very hard on ways to improve the standard of living of his people. After the exile in England, Seretse and Ruth, with their four young children, returned to his home village in Bechuanaland. He organized the legislature and rose rapidly in the local power structure. It was the 1960s and the British authorities were aware of the sweep of independence and were prepared to facilitate the movement for self-government when they had confidence in the local leadership. This was true with Seretse Khama. His dedication to ending the unholy Trinity of poverty, illiteracy, and disease soon made him a popular hero among the local people.

When Khama and his family returned to the then Bechuana-land, the situation for a country as large as France was bleak. Livestock rearing engaged 90 percent of the population and represented 75 percent of the national income. With his quiet determination, Khama, initiated the economic changes that transformed Botswana into one of the countries in the world with the fastest growth rates.

While promoting the establishment of the government ma-chinery and working with British colonial leadership, Khama never hesitated to speak against racial discrimination and to advocate reconciliation. For many observers this was a coura-geous political act in the face of the strong apartheid position of his next-door neighbor, the Republic of South Africa. He was committed and strongly engaged but carefully avoided any manifestation of emotional extremism.

At a meeting of the board of trustees of Africa Service Insti-tute in 1963, Tom was encouraged to visit Bechuanaland and to establish contact with Khama. John Mosler, a trustee of the Institute who had never visited Africa, wanted to accompany Tom on his visit. Tom began the process of contacting the Bechuanaland government in Gaborone, where Khama was living with his family.

Tom's book *White Man's Future in Black Africa* was published in 1962. A paperback, it was well received by the media and resulted in many media interviews for Tom. He wrote the book during our courtship, and he took a very strong position on the evils of racism so prevalent then in southern Africa and especially in the Republic of South Africa.

We had visited the Republic of South Africa in 1962 before the book was published. It was a very meaningful experience for both of us. Margaret's college classmate, Jean Gallagher, had been there for a year and was a great guide. She arranged visits for us with all racial groups.

Our visit with Archbishop Dennis Hurley, the head of the Catholic Archdiocese of Durban, resulted in the South African police starting a file on us. We had met the archbishop at conferences in the United States and admired his strong position against racial discrimination. He organized a dinner for us and the guest list included white, colored, black, and Indian lay people. We were consequently able to explore the topics of racial reconciliation with laymen and laywomen going through the experience of living in the apartheid country of South Africa. It was also a source of comfort for us that the very meaningful evening was sponsored by a Catholic church leader.

The combination of Tom's book and the police file on our 1962 visit to South Africa caused Tom problems when he went to Gaborone with John Mosler. Many of the customs and police officers in 1962 were South Africans and their main source of information about us was in the files of the South African police.

During our three days in Gaborone, Tom enjoyed the hospitality of the Paulist Fathers, a community of American Catholic missionary priests. They attempted to assist Tom in obtaining access to Seretse, who was traveling in the country. We were to learn later that delaying tactics followed by the police kept Tom and John Mosler from seeing him on that visit. Tom ended by leaving a letter for Seretse. The missionary priests and sisters who generously provided hospitality were lavish in their praise of Khama as a stable leader. It was also evident that, given the apartheid attitude of total separation in the neighboring state, the interracial marriage of Seretse Khama and Ruth Williams with four happy children was a welcome contrast.

When Tom returned to the United States he phoned Wayne Fredericks in the Bureau of African Affairs of the U.S. Department of State and related to him the lack of cooperation of the custom and border officials in Bechuanaland. He looked into the matter and later reported that Tom would have difficulty with South African associated police, as he was regarded as too pro-African independence and was simultaneously critical of South African racial policies.

The discussions with the American missionaries in Gaborone led Tom to see Bishop Edward Swanstrom, head of Catholic Relief Services (CRS), when he returned to New York. CRS had a program of assistance for developing societies. Bishop Swanstrom moved quickly and sent Monsignor Wilson Kaiser to meet with Seretse Khama, by this time prime minister of

Bechuanaland. It was a remarkable example of the private sector taking a leading position in promoting economic development. The primary purpose in the early 1960s of the CRS operation in Africa was to provide assistance for the refugees.

Botswana: Nonracial and Unified

Seretse Khama's effective leadership and the desire of the British colonial leadership to facilitate an orderly change converged. The rapidly moving political situation culminated in 1966 when full sovereign independence was granted on September 30 and Bechuanaland became Botswana.

In 1965 Seretse had hinted in a letter to Tom that 1966 would be the "big year" for full sovereign independence for his country. We wanted the leadership of Seretse Khama — both his political leadership and his campaign for racial reconciliation — to be recognized before the recognition that would occur once he became chief of state.

We presented this recommendation for an honorary doctorate of laws degree for Seretse to the president of Fordham University in the spring of 1965. He acted quickly and we informed Seretse. It became a matter of Seretse's calendar and when he could absent himself from Bechuanaland. The date was established as October 25, 1965, and he would bring his wife, Ruth, with him. We were very pleased, as we wanted the world to see a happy, successful biracial couple.

Since the degree would be conferred at a special academic convocation, we prepared a list of U.N. ambassadors, government, civic, and academic leaders who would be invited. We

Seretse Khama with Father Leo J. McLaughlin, President of Fordham University, in 1966

were consulted about the citation. It acknowledged the significant role that Seretse Khama played in directing the strategy for obtaining independence. Since the convocation took place at a time when the assumption was that independence was "just around the corner," there was a very pleasant atmosphere of anticipation at the convocation ceremony. Our goal was through example and encouragement to inspire interracial harmony. The convocation was a moving tribute to a man dedicated to achieving the goal by rapid evolutionary change. In a brief and strong tone of executive leadership, the prime minister proudly declared in his speech, "My ideal is to establish a democratic state which must also be completely nonracial and unified." (The full text of the speech is included as Appendix 3, beginning on page 185 below.)

We wanted Seretse Khama to receive the full treatment and honors normally given to visiting European heads of government. The evening following the convocation John Mosler, a trustee of the Africa Service Institute, and his wife gave a formal dinner party for Seretse Khama and his wife, Ruth. This social event was attended by many of the city's social leaders.

The Khamas remained in the country for a few days and made some new contacts that would assist him in pushing his country forward. We had informed the African Studies Association about his visit. He was the keynote speaker at their conference on October 28.

Tom saw Seretse again several days after the Fordham convocation. He related how he was working with British government officials to complete the final steps to full sovereign independence. He told Tom that he expected the event would be in the fall of 1966.

We were both later invited by formal invitation. With one small child we were not able to participate in the independence events scheduled for September 29–October 2, 1966, in Gaborone. On September 29 we were at a restaurant and saluted him for his success in the founding of a state free of racial discrimination in southern Africa.

Within a few years it was evident that Seretse Khama was guiding the rapid economic growth of the newly founded

Botswana. At the same time he became a powerful symbol of racial reconciliation. He did this while his neighbors in the Republic of South Africa continued their efforts to maintain a system of racial inequality. The success of the system of racial equality in Botswana was a factor leading to the collapse of the system of racial inequality in South Africa. It was a significant change in human behavior, and Seretse Khama played a role in achieving the change from white minority control in southern Africa to majority rule.

When Seretse died in July 1980, his legacy was fully established. We were then at Sacred Heart University in Fairfield, Connecticut, where Tom was president. We remembered the note with his last Christmas card. We had also heard from others that having won the struggle for independence, he was losing the battle against cancer.

Books about Seretse Khama

Dutfield, Michael. *A Marriage of Inconvenience: Persecution of Ruth and Seretse Khama.* London: Unwin Hyman, 1990.

Mungazi, Dickson. *We Shall Not Fail: Values in the National Leadership of Seretse Khama, Nelson Mandela and Julius Nyerere.* Princeton, N.J.: Africa World Press, 2005.

Seager, Alan. *The Shadow of a Great Rock.* Flintshire, England: Connah's Quay, I & D Books, 2004.

Parsons, Neil, Willie Henderson, and Thomas Tlou. *Seretse Khama, 1921–1980.* Braamfontein: Macmillan, 1995.

Williams, Susan. *Colour Bar: The Triumph of Seretse Khama and His Nation.* London: Allen Lane, 2006.

Chapter Five

THOMAS JOSEPH MBOYA
Young Kenyan in a Hurry

A meeting in London with a young man from Kenya in May 1959 gave Tom the impression that the young, energetic, well organized, smiling man from the land of Mau Mau would have a key role in the emerging drama of black Africa. His road to leadership took a different turn from that of Senghor, Nyerere, and Khama. He was not the son of a tribal chief or an heir, like Seretse Khama, to a royal throne. He did not, like Senghor or Nyerere, indicate an interest in university studies or in different philosophies. Tom Mboya chose to pursue a trade, and beginning with his early experience as a sanitary inspector, he appreciated the value of a work ethic as well as the effectiveness of an organized worker movement.

Mboya's early years took place at the end of the failed policy to continue colonial white settler control. He experienced the sting of racial discrimination both as a resident of Kenya and personally. At the age of twenty, following graduation from the Royal Sanitary Institutes Medical Training School in Nairobi for sanitary inspectors, he started work in a village. It was 1950. His first job in the inspector department lasted a few months. His white colleagues never acknowledged his reports or his presence.

On one occasion when the European boss was absent, an English woman seeking a dairy license brought in a sample of milk for inspection. Her comment when she saw Tom Mboya was, "Is there anybody here?" Mboya understood the implication that an African was not "somebody" who could handle her request.

He was still young, and fortunately his early education was in a Christian spiritual milieu, at mission schools operated by Irish Catholic priests. He was an earnest young man, and his studies at the Holy Ghost College earned him a Cambridge School Certificate. The American and Irish missionaries assigned to Kenya inspired him. The missionaries remained and carried out their educational mission during the violence that took place in the post–World War II period in Kenya. Their presence and courage gave him another point of view — the world was not all racist.

In his teen years he also clearly indicated an interest in public affairs. He engaged in debating and received a scholarship for Ruskin College, Oxford, where he made many trade union contacts. The fast-moving life of Tom Mboya coincided with the sweep of independence of the 1960s. It came to a closure at the end of that decade when he was assassinated in the city of Nairobi.

The Airlift

The election of Barack Obama as the forty-fourth president of the United States in 2008 sparked new interest in the life of Tom Mboya. President Obama's father, Barack Obama Sr., was a

U.S.-educated Kenyan who benefited from Mboya's scholarship program in the 1960s. In 1959 Mboya organized his well-known Airlift Africa. With the assistance of the African American Students Foundation, eighty-one Kenyan students were flown to the United States to pursue studies at American colleges and universities. This was the first of many such flights of Kenyan students. Barack Obama Sr. was one of the Kenyan students who went to Hawaii for his university studies. We witnessed all of the controversy in African-U.S. circles about the advisability of the airlift. Numerous questions were raised about the students' qualifications. We remember meeting young Kenyans in New York. They were always full of enthusiasm when they talked about the airlift and the college that they would be attending. While we knew that there might be some weaknesses in their preparation, we both felt that sustained enthusiasm would assist in bridging the gap.

In the end, the airlift must be declared a success as it opened higher education to the future leadership class of Kenyan. It was similar to President Franklin Roosevelt's establishment of the G.I. Bill of Rights, which opened the possibility of a higher education to millions of Americans who otherwise would not have had the opportunity. Tom Melady was also a beneficiary of the G.I. Bill. Only one parent of his had an eighth-grade diploma, and we clearly believed that the benefit he received through the G.I. Bill (the bachelor's degree and most of the master's degree) gave him an excellent exit from the working class to the professional group of university graduates. Tom Melady has always been enthusiastic about extending the opportunities of access for higher education to as many people as possible.

Senator John F. Kennedy with Kenyan leader Thomas Mboya.

Within a few months of the first airlift (1959), Tom Mboya met with the then Senator John Kennedy. Following their contact, the prestigious Kennedy Foundation underwrote the costs of the airlifts. In 1960 alone, 230 Kenyan students came to the United States through the Africa airlift. It continued for several years with another several hundred Kenyan students receiving scholarships to study at American institutions. This one association with the Kennedy family was a great asset for Mboya in his U.S. contacts.

The airlift combined with Mboya's natural speaking skills gave him the influence to move rapidly upward once Kenya received its independence in 1963. He was elected as an MP

from the Nairobi constituency. His first position in the government was as minister of justice and constitutional affairs. later
he was minister for economic planning and development.

Our Relationship with Tom Mboya

Mboya indicated several times to Tom his admiration for Israel's
economic assistance program for Africa. Tom, in his 1965 visit
to Africa, first went to Israel to see for himself. Starting June 21,
he was the guest of the ministry of foreign affairs. The Director of their Africa bureau briefed Tom on the overall goal of
their African assistance. With limited resources, the Israelis
concentrated on programs that would improve the living standards and could be carried out by Africans. Tom then had
three days packed full of conferences with top Israeli officials
on African political and technical assistance matters. Tom was
quite impressed with the quality of their programs from both
the political and human points of view.

Tom Melady's initial contacts were with a young man of
twenty. One was as already described at a hotel in London.
The other was in New York City when Mboya was the guest
of Theodore Kheel, prominent labor attorney and influential in
the Democratic Party. U.S. labor union leaders and those active
in Democratic Party activities attended the lunch. Tom Melady
was introduced to Mboya as a person active in Catholic affairs.
Mboya responded by saying that he attended a Catholic school
in Kenya and that he was Catholic.

Tom later wrote to Mboya and saw him during his 1961–63
visits to the United States. It soon became evident that he was

close to the international activists of the AFL-CIO. When he was in New York he operated out of the office of Irving Brown, who directed the African American Labor Center across the street from the United Nations. Brown was an excellent contact for Mboya with the Johnson administration.

The first part of Mboya's career brought him into contact with the Cold War. The U.S. labor movement, especially the American Federation of Labor, was a major player in Europe and other parts of the world against Soviet-connected communism.

Under the leadership of Irving Brown, the African American Labor Center provided assistance to the free trade unions in Africa. Brown was active in the 1950s and 1960s in leading the labor union opposition to the Communist Party's alliance with the trade union movements in Europe and North Africa.

Catholic Connections

Our relationship with Tom Mboya almost exclusively focused on Catholic-related matters. In all of our conversations we indicated that we would assist him in areas where he needed contacts. Tom actually turned to Mboya, who had associations with Goans and others of Portuguese-connected backgrounds when he was serving in the Kenya Legislative Council. On June 16, 1961, Tom wrote to Mboya about the situation in Angola. In all our contacts with the African leaders we urged them, notwithstanding their own struggles, to engage the challenges of the Portuguese colonies in Africa.

We had heard on a stopover visit with Vatican friends that Tom Mboya was known as a Catholic layman concerned about issues of development. We sent him both a full copy of the encyclical "The Development of Peoples" and our own analysis.

Mboya responded on April 18, 1967. He reported to Tom what he had previously said, "we need a program of actions.... Expressions of hope cannot fill the bellies of hungry men and so long as this situation exists world peace cannot be achieved." Tom Mboya was always thoughtful, but he wanted action, a fact that was present for the rest of his short life.

In 1967, we were campaigning for a strong papal statement on racism. On September 6, Tom wrote to Mboya urging him to join the campaign and to be in direct contact with Pope Paul VI through Archbishop del Mestri, the papal envoy in Nairobi.

In June 1967, the Holy See released its proposal for an International Regime in Jerusalem. Monsignor Alberto Giovanetti, the Permanent Observer of the Holy See to the United Nations, had spoken to Tom about seeking support from African states for the Holy See's plan that in 1967 differed on some aspects from that of Israel. Mboya responded with enthusiasm about supporting the initiative of the Holy See.

Mboya stayed in touch with Tom from time to time with regard to Catholic matters. On October 2, 1967, he wrote a long letter on his personal stationery. After discussing his relationship with Archbishop del Mestri, the papal envoy in Nairobi, he wrote:

> Perhaps at this point I might raise with you something that has bothered me personally a lot. There has been considerable discussion within the Catholic Church of a number of very important questions. At the same time the

Pope has become increasingly involved in a lot of problems facing the world. There are two things which worry me about this development:

One is that certain of the assumptions that have been regarded as reflecting world trends are those that concern only the very small articulate group of critics of and in the Church. There is really no measure by which one can determine what the layman is thinking, and the relations between the Church and the laity have, I think, not really been on a basis that would facilitate such expression! Are we not running the risk of turning the Church into just another social organization? Or even worse still the place where intellectuals carry out a theological debate in an attempt to speak for the "people." I understand, of course, that the world scene has changed and that the Church must respond to the new developments. It is also true that the Church needs to have influence over some of the changes that are taking place. I think, however, that there are certain things that need to be preserved, and which create the image of the Church in the minds of the people. After all, the most important relationship here must continue to be based on Faith and not just good citizenship.

He then went on to point out the differences unfolding in the worldwide situation for the church:

It is also necessary to appreciate that most of the population of the world do not live within the articulate group to be found in Europe and North America. Sudden changes in the structure of the Church can only lead to serious doubts being raised in the minds of the millions of laymen who cannot follow the debate that is taking place. Let me hasten to state that I am not here thinking of things like the debate on contraception. I myself believe firmly that the Church will have to revise its thinking on this sensitive subject. What I have in mind are things like the recent decision to give up the use of Latin in celebrating the Mass, and the change in the physical arrangements within the Church such as the place of the altar and so on. The Universality of the Church is an important part of its image. The ability of priests to go into any church and say Mass is important in this respect, and I am afraid that some of the changes that are being introduced will confuse rather than help people to understand the Church. Welfare activities, including the social groups within the Church, should carry out the functions that relate to changing societies in which we live; I think the Church proper needs to be preserved as far as possible as it always has been.

Concluding his letter, Mboya observed various international political facts concerning the pope,

My second point relates to the Pope as the Head of the Church. It is encouraging that the Pope has been able to visit various countries in the recent years, but I must confess that I am doubtful that he should be brought into every dispute that takes place in the world, or that he should be required to make political statements on every issue that faces the world. Sooner or later people will begin to ask what is his influence and sooner or later he may have to take a stand as a logical sequence of the decision or to be involved and to make statements on various issues and developments in the world. To pray for peace is something which he must do in the name of the Church, but to pronounce on Viet Nam or on the Congo in a political context is hardly part of his role as Head of the Church.

We discussed these issues raised by Mboya. Tom especially looked forward to discussing the issues personally with Mboya, as Mboya challenged him:

I realize that by these remarks I may have provoked you into a reaction, and I would welcome that, for I would like to debate these issues with somebody such as you.

Tom Melady responded to Tom Mboya, who said that he expected to be in Washington in the summer for an appointment with President Nixon, but the conversation on these issues never took place as a Nairobi gunman silenced the voice of this thoughtful Catholic layman.

U.S. Political Scene

As Republicans we were active in the preparation for the 1968 presidential elections. We both attended the Republican convention in Miami, as we were active on behalf of Governor Nelson A. Rockefeller. Tom was especially pleased with Rockefeller's position on Africa and wrote position papers for him on Africa and the third world. We were with Nelson Rockefeller at his hotel suite when he learned that he was defeated at the convention by Richard M. Nixon. The governor thanked us for our support and urged that we be active in the presidential campaign on behalf of Richard M. Nixon.

Tom had corresponded with Mboya on the implications of the election on the U.S. foreign policy in Africa. On February 6, 1969, Tom Mboya wrote to Tom saying, "I look forward to hearing from you on the ideas you have regarding President Nixon." Tom responded, indicating that he checked with friends at the White House and there would not be any problem with him seeing the president. They agreed to meet in August 1969 in New York City where they could continue their discussion on the church.

Their meeting never occurred. He was gunned down on July 5, 1969, on a street in Nairobi. He was thirty-nine. On July 15 at 5:00 p.m., friends of Tom Mboya living in the United States attended a Mass in his memory at the Holy Family Church near the United Nations.

Books by and about
Thomas Joseph Mboya

Mboya, Tom. *Freedom and After*. Boston: Little Brown, 1963.

———. *The Challenge of Nationhood: A Collection of Speeches and Writings*. Foreword by Jomo Kenyatta. Postscript by Pamela Mboya. New York: Praeger, 1970.

Evans Boyte, Sara. *Tom Mboya of Kenya: A Case Study of the Interaction of Politics and Ideology in Emerging Africa*. Durham, N.C.: Duke University Press, 1968.

Goldsworthy, David. *Tom Mboya: The Man Kenya Wanted to Forget*. Nairobi: Heinemann, 1982.

Chapter Six

HOLDEN ROBERTO
Angolan Patriot

November 21, 1963, was a typical late fall day in New York City, but our experiences that day were nothing short of extraordinary. We were in our apartment when we received a phone call. On the other end of the line was Holden Roberto; he had just arrived at Idlewild airport (later named after President John F. Kennedy). However, this was not a friendly phone call to say he had arrived safely. In fact, it was quite the opposite. Holden was in pain from a gunshot wound inflicted upon him in Tunis during an attempted assassination. We offered him our assistance and recommended he check himself in at Columbia Hospital. The hospital was close to our apartment, and we could easily see him there. In an ironic switching of roles, it was Holden who eased our concerns by reassuring us that although he had a serious injury, it was not life threatening. We met him at the hospital and he registered under another name, as he did not want anyone except us to know about the episode.

The following day we visited him in the hospital. Visiting hospitals can often be taxing to one's soul, and this particular visit would more than adhere to that principle. Entering his room, we were startled to see Roberto sobbing. Here, in front of us, a hardened African revolutionary was incapacitated. He was not crying from the wound in his leg. In a moment of awareness, our attention was drawn to a stream of French blaring from the speakers of a radio in the room. Roberto was listening to the Brazzaville radio station. President Kennedy had been shot. He was dead. We were overwhelmed to say the least. In between gasps Roberto informed us that he was expecting to see the president. We assumed his good friend Joseph Mobutu of the Congo facilitated this appointment. Of course I knew that Roberto had very close ties with other members of the U.S. government, including the Department of State.

His discontent was very apparent. We knew that from previous discussions with him that he was a great admirer of President Kennedy. Their association traced back to a time when, as a U.S. Senator, Kennedy was a member of the U.S. Senate Committee on Foreign Relations with a responsibility for the Subcommittee on African Affairs.

For the next few days, time stood still for our nation. We divided our time between our apartment, riveted to the television watching plans unfold for the state funeral and keeping touch with Holden's progress at the hospital. When Holden was released, we took him to our apartment, where we spent the entire day watching the funeral and burial of our U.S. president. We all, including Holden, reflected on this tragic moment in U.S. history, but also on the strength of a nation to persevere. For Holden, who had just survived an assassination attempt, it was particularly poignant, not only because of his personal brush with death, but also because of the consequences for the future of a free Angola.

Holden Roberto was a true Angolan patriot. He sacrificed his mind, body, and soul for the freedom of his homeland. We were fortunate enough to have seen him several times a year from 1960 until 1968 and consequently established a strong relationship. When Tom was appointed ambassador to Burundi in 1969 we restricted our contact. However, we were both simultaneously aware of Holden's activities through letters, word of mouth, and the general chatter of the then small U.S. community active in African affairs. The President Kennedy story is just one of many encounters we shared. Each time he visited the United States in the 1960s he would visit us. From the beginning of our association with Holden, we assumed that he would lead Angola to independence. Tom was convinced that the historic sweep of independence that became apparent in 1960 could spread soon to all of Africa, including the Portuguese colonies. The French, British, and Belgian governments appreciated the reality of the sweep in Africa, which was fundamentally taking place without violence. Holden was inspired by these developments and believed that the government of Portugal could be persuaded to initiate the process of orderly change in their African territories. The Portuguese were mostly products of a Catholic culture, but in Angola the Protestant missionaries had succeeded in educating many black Africans. Holden Roberto had been born into a Protestant Christian family, and even though he succeeded in entering the Portuguese civil service in Angola, he was never comfortable with the Portuguese culture. So Tom turned to Catholic and Protestant leaders.

We were not the only Americans Roberto had contacted. He was willing to contact anyone he could to help his people, but our association with Roberto was especially focused on relief efforts.

The Christian ecumenical community responded quickly and enthusiastically to Tom's suggestion of making an appeal. The Rev. Dr. Theodore L. Tucker, secretary of the Africa Committee of the National Council of Churches, worked closely with Tom and hosted several organizational meetings at their office at 475 Riverside Drive in New York City.

An impressive group of over eighty Protestant and Catholic leaders signed the statement, which was issued at a press conference on June 5, 1961. (The work on this Angolan project coincided with our becoming serious with one another. We had been dating for about three months. We were together at the press conference on June 5, four days before we became engaged on June 9, 1961.)

The statement began by pointing out, "concern for the recent developments in Angola. It called for the government of Portugal to initiate the process of change in the African territories of Angola, Mozambique, and Portuguese Guinea." It concluded with a relatively mild statement, "We believe that these changes can only be achieved through consultation with the representatives of the African people. To be effective they must incorporate the desires of the Africans themselves, including especially a rapidly increasing participation in the process of government." (The full text of the statement is included as Appendix 1, beginning on page 171.)

The U.S. and Western media coverage was significant. The editorial reaction of the American and Western European media was very favorable. We both believed that this would initiate a

rapid change in the policy of Portugal and that it would essentially follow the example of France. But it took much longer and
resulted in more suffering and bloodshed in Angola and other
African territories of Portugal.

The appeal was made in 1961. The results were a disappointment for us and for all who believed that the millions living
in African colonies should have also benefited from the 1960
sweep of independence in black Africa. The Angolan people
waited until 1975, fifteen years after the 1960 sweep.

Shortly after the June 1961 press conference and our engagement on June 9, Tom made his final preparations for a trip to
Africa. Tops on the list were stops in the two neighboring states
of Congo and Zambia to assess the situation of the Angolan
refugees. Friends in the Department of State advised Tom not
to attempt a visit to any Portuguese territory in Africa, as Portuguese police would have a file on him. It was known that staff of
the Mission of Portugal to the United Nations had an "observer"
at the press conference.

Margaret remained in New York while Tom made his 1961
summer trip to Africa. During these three months when she
was not making plans for our marriage, Margaret assisted at the
Africa Service Institute (ASI), office which was given tempo-
rary quarters at the National Council of Churches building at
475 Riverside Drive. ASI had grown to the point where it also
needed a director. Ron Davidson, a recent graduate of Fordham
University who was a student active in the Catholic interracial
movement and waiting for the results of his Foreign Service
application, was appointed interim Director.

Visit inside Angola

Our association with Holden Roberto and with others from Angola led us to observe that his family roots had a royal lineage, which gave him an added status with the Angolans who were seeking independence from the rule of Portugal.

His tactics for obtaining his goal emphasized engagement at a broad local level. He developed very close ties with the African political leadership in neighboring Congo and Zambia. He also maintained contact with Portuguese officials

The same was true with his American contacts. He had connections with the Department of State and with a number of private organizations and people who could be helpful in one way or another with his efforts on behalf of the Angolan people. One such person was Dr. John Marcum, a leading American academic specializing in Africa.

During the same years in the 1960s we heard comments that portrayed Roberto as content to sit back in the Congo and let others do his fighting for him in Angola. Tom wanted to evaluate the situation within Angola. After a year of weighing the impact of the 1961 appeal to the government of Portugal, it was painfully evident to us that the struggle for independence in Angola would not immediately benefit from the 1960 sweep of independence in black Africa.

Holden made the arrangements for Tom to visit a revolutionary camp within Angola. Tom advised his contacts at the U.S. Embassy in Kinshasa and received a neutral response; neither a firm "you should not do it," nor a mild approval. Tom decided that he would do it.

Tom's main reason was to observe the culture and morale of an Angolan camp within the boundaries of Angola. Tom was also aware of the implications of repeated rumors that Roberto preferred engagement with leaders abroad as opposed to being at the battlefront himself. Tom wanted to see what the situation was among the warriors living and fighting within the country. What was their opinion of Holden?

It was a hot and sticky afternoon in July 1962 when Tom, Holden, and six of Holden's colleagues left for the Angolan border. Another group of young men, who were all armed, met them. Holden speaking first in Portuguese, then for Tom's benefit in English, instructed the group on a few rules. Tom remembered two essential themes: Be very quiet, no noise, and stay close to Holden.

They arrived at the camp early the following morning. The local revolutionary camp leaders formally greeted Holden in military style. They later engaged in military drill exercises. During the midday break Tom, through an interpreter, discussed what their goal was; what they wanted: It was clear: independence. Furthermore, they knew that significant developments were occurring in other parts of Africa. In a sense they knew that a sweep of change was occurring. They wanted to be a part of it.

Tom followed instructions as they exited Angola and did not say one word. But he was able to reflect on the overall implications of the Angolan situation. Tom told Margaret that he believed that the road ahead to independence for the Angolans would take a route different from Senegal, Tanzania, and Zambia. Tom began to say that the road to independence for Angola would be longer and more difficult than it was for the former British, French, and Belgian colonies.

In the meantime, we both completely believed that it was in the best interests of the United States to become identified and assist the Angolans with their movement for independence. There was never any question for us that it was the morally correct action for us to support in every way that we could.

Assistance for Suzanne Roberto

Holden had spoken to us about his wife, Suzanne, and frankly told us that Suzanne needed to upgrade her education in the French language to prepare for her future duties. When Margaret met her in Kinshasa, Suzanne indicated her wish to study at the level of a high school. With the assistance of a grant from Henry Leir through his company, Margaret arranged for her to have a year of courses at a school in Lausanne, Switzerland. In the summer of 1964, Margaret stayed in France while Tom traveled to Africa. She arranged to visit Suzanne in Lausanne for a weekend and then she invited Suzanne to visit Paris. Margaret continued to correspond with Suzanne, who never failed to thank us for the assistance she received. In October, when Margaret attended the independence ceremonies in Zambia, she met Holden and reported on Suzanne's progress. Holden was genuinely pleased and appreciative. When Suzanne was preparing to leave for Africa, she wrote in French to Margaret saying how "her studies had been very worthwhile" and asked me to tell Tom of her "deep gratitude" for having made possible her stay in Switzerland.

Thomas Melady talking with Holden Roberto in Kinshasa, August 1963.
Source: Photo by Margaret Melady

Later in Holden's career, he separated from Suzanne and later married the sister of President Mobutu of the Congo. The marriage into the Mobutu family gave the appearance of a move made for political reasons. In this situation, as with others, we deliberately refrained from indicating pleasure or disappointment with the personal actions of an African leader.

One reason for this was our sensitivity to the historical fact that the sweep of independence in the 1960s was following at least a century of European domination where the "white man" was frequently using expressions of racial superiority to describe the actions of African people. Divorce and marriage for political advantage was not uncommon among Europeans and Americans. We never commented on the matter.

The Angolan Refugees

Numerous Angolan refugees had fled to the Congo. We decided that our efforts to help the independence movement would focus on assisting the refugees with their desperate need for food, clothes, and medical supplies. Following an appeal from Holden in 1961 for us to encourage the relief agencies, Tom, after discussing the matter with White House staff, sent the following appeal to President Kennedy on April 20, 1961:

Holden Roberto, President of the Union of the Populations of Angola, and I met with Mr. James Norris of Catholic Relief Services in New York City to discuss an urgent problem of feeding around 25,000 Angolan refugees in the

Hatadi area of Congo. It is imperative that food, medical, clothing, and shelter be provided to Angolan refugees. I respectfully request that the U.S. Embassy in Leopoldville be alerted to render appropriate assistance to Catholic Relief Services and other groups who wish to assist Angolan refugees. Mr. Roberto sends his appreciation and best wishes.

The response of the church-related relief agencies to the pressing Angolan needs was very good. Tom, in the 1961–68 period, met on a regular basis with heads of Catholic Relief Services, Lutheran World Relief, Church World Service, and other groups.

By the summer of 1963, African Service Institute had helped Holden to set up a medical clinic for the Angolan refugees in Kinshasa. A Haitian doctor had been recruited to run the clinic. When we arrived in Kinshasa to check on the clinic, we were surprised that the refugees had placed our last name, "Melady," as the name of the clinic. Margaret observed an operation performed at the clinic and took photos to document the clinic's work for the U.S. donors to the project. During that same visit in 1963, Holden arranged for us to visit a camp on the Congolese-Angolan border. It was a grueling trip in a Jeep on barely passable roads to a camp set in the African bush. We were given the only hut and bed in the small village, and the next morning we observed some of the operations at the military staging area. Back in Leopoldville (now Kinshasa), Margaret established contact with the Association of Angolan Women, which she continued to assist until we left

New York and prepared for our Embassy assignment in Burundi. In a letter written to Margaret in 1968, the Angolan women reported, "Everything seems to be going on wonderfully with our movement. Some Catholic Fathers visited our social center last September and they surely were amazed to see what we have accomplished so far." We were very pleased that we were involving both Catholic organizations and clergy in helping the Angolan refugees.

In a December 1966 letter, Holden acknowledged a medical shipment, especially the penicillin. Tom knew that we were approaching the completion of the work of ASI, and so in 1966–68 he gave emphasis to maximizing the shipment of medical supplies, clothes, and food supplements to Angola.

As we began to plan our future in 1967, Tom alerted Holden in a letter that we were looking forward to a more traditional academic career. Little did we know that the full academic career would last for a year, and Tom would then be appointed a U.S. ambassador. Tom included that information in a note to Holden congratulating him and his colleagues on the sixth anniversary of the Angolan revolution. Holden responded in a letter on April 14, 1967, to Tom:

I have just received your gentle letter of March 22, 1967, wherein you are congratulating me for the success of our commemoration of the 6th anniversary of our just cause.

Believe it Tom, when such congratulations come from a friend like you, they get very touching because, I know that they are sincere and heartly. I have passed your letter over all my collaborators and, like me, they have all felt the genuineness of your congratulations. I am indeed, hereafter, sending two copies of *Progres*, a local journal reporting on that manifestation.

Tom, though I have not been able to be with you for long time, you remain always within my heart. I hope to take advantage of a U.N. session this year and expect to see you then. My best regards to Margaret.

I hope also that your newly edited book *Western Policy and the Third World* will be a success. I am very anxious to get a copy as soon as it is available.

During this period we made several trips to the Congo in order to see President Mobutu and also to Zambia in order to call on President Kaunda. Our basic message was for them to facilitate and support in every way possible the arrival of relief supplies to the Angolan refugee camps within their countries. The critical necessities were always the same: medicines (especially penicillin), clothing, blankets, and food supplements. Catholic Relief Services, as a result of an annual national campaign, had a large supply of clean secondhand clothing. Thousands of Angolan refugees in the 1960s were clothed by the aid provided by CRS.

Changing Relationship

When Tom completed his work at the Africa Service Institute and started full-time teaching at Seton Hall University in 1968, the contacts with Holden began to diminish. When Tom was appointed ambassador to Burundi in 1969, we heard from Holden only at Christmas time.

Angola became independent in 1975. As the independence period developed, Roberto played a significant role in the new nation-state. Although Roberto never achieved his ambition of becoming the chief of state, he proved to be a patient participant in the nation building and accepted his role as the head of the opposition.

Influenced as he was by the Protestant tradition, being the son of a minister, Roberto first experienced the great challenge of seeking to establish a dialogue with the Portuguese, the original colonists of Angola. He easily emerged into a contemporary revolutionary role. He sought and received assistance from the U.S. government agencies, relief organizations, and foundations.

His final years were in the capital of Luanda. He died a natural death at the age of eighty-four in August 2007. We were among his admirers and regretted that circumstances prevented us from attending the farewell ceremonies in Luanda.

Both Holden Roberto and Eduardo Mondlane, the Mozambique revolutionary leader, were influenced in their early youth by Protestant teachings. They faced the Portuguese colonial system which, unlike the British, French, and Belgium governments, refused to participate in the 1960s sweep of independence. The recognition came in 1975 after extensive suffering and death in both countries.

Books about Holden Roberto

Hamann, Hilton. *Days of the Generals.* Cape Town: Zebra, 2001.

James, W. Martin, and Susan H. Broadhead. *Historical Dictionary of Angola.* Lanham, Md.: Scarecrow Press, 2004.

Lamb, David. *The Africans.* New York: Vintage Books, 1987.

Van Rensburg, Abraham Paul Janse. *Contemporary Leaders of Africa.* Cape Town: Haum, 1975.

Current Biography. New York: H. W. Wilson Company, 1991, page 499.

Chapter Seven

EDUARDO C. MONDLANE
Martyr for Mozambique

As Tom became active in African affairs in New York City in 1961, he was frequently told that he should meet Eduardo C. Mondlane, a leader from Mozambique who was campaigning for a political change in his country. Tom contacted him and arranged for a luncheon on May 11, 1961. He did not resemble the usual African liberation leader. Dr. Eduardo Mondlane had received all his university degrees from American universities. Tom was greatly impressed by the way Eduardo handled the initial meeting, during which they had a general discussion about the world situation and how it applied to Mozambique.

It was May 1961 and Tom had initiated a campaign to influence the government of Portugal because he felt that all of the European countries with African colonies should participate in the sweep for independence that was overtaking most of black Africa. France, England, and Belgium had responded both to the idealism of recognizing the human right for people to determine their status and also to the political realities that independence was just around the corner. However, Portugal was holding out. Tom believed that a group of centrist Americans of the

Protestant and Catholic churches could push for the process of change.

He communicated all of this enthusiasm to Eduardo, who did not join Tom in the belief that the Portuguese government would modify its historical position on the Portuguese colonies in Africa. Following the lunch on May 11, he mailed to Tom an eleven-page statement on present conditions in Mozambique. Although Eduardo was an attractive and charismatic leader, he did not endorse Tom's position. He felt that it would take increasing political pressure by the United States to obtain a significant change in the Portuguese position. The day after their May 11 luncheon, Tom was impressed with the follow-up memo from Eduardo. In his memo he emphasized the following goals for the United States:

> The people of Mozambique think that the United States believes in justice for all of humanity. When the issue of Angola was discussed in the last session of the General Assembly and in the Security Council, the part played by the American delegation convinced the Africans that the United States meant to carry out its oft-expressed sentiments of sympathy with the oppressed peoples of the world. They also appreciated the courage with which Mr. G. Mennen Williams enunciated the principle that the United States wanted for Africans only what the Africans wanted for themselves. They interpreted it to mean that no enclaves of powers outside of Africa should continue to exist against the will of the African peoples. *However, unless these expressions of sympathy are followed by immediate*

action, African people may begin to doubt the firmness of that resolve. Other powers have expressed similar sentiments, perhaps with different intent. However, they seem eager to help. It would be better that our fight against Portugal be interpreted as the struggle for freedom, and not the Cold War between the East and the West. This does not mean that we are not concerned with the ideological struggle between Capitalism and Communism. Indeed we are. But at this moment the fight against colonialism absorbs all our attention. If our independence were to come peacefully, we might find time to consider the advantages and disadvantages of either politico-economic system. At this moment, however, we must devote all our attention to the immediate problem: ridding ourselves of the arbitrary rule by a foreign power.

The United States of America has several advantageous points from which she could act as mediator between the Portuguese Government and the African peoples.

- She has long-standing friendship with Portugal, exemplified by the many treaties of friendship and mutual aid that exist between the two countries.

- It seems as though the United States does not have as many good economic interests in Portuguese Africa as some of the Western European powers, so that she stands much less chance to suffer from economic sanctions by Portugal.

- Both the United States and Portugal are allies in the North Atlantic Treaty Organization, which is

committed to fight for free governments everywhere in
the world.

- Portugal depends almost totally upon the United States
  for her military strength (in 1960 Portugal received
  nearly $17 million in military aid).

- Portugal relies upon the United States for economic
  development (in 1960 economic aid from the United
  States to Portugal amounted to more than $25 million).

These, plus many more relationships of which I may not
be aware, represent ties between the two countries that
should facilitate their communication. It would appear,
therefore, that the United States would be in a position to:

a. encourage Portugal to accept the principle of self-
   determination for the African peoples under her
   control;

b. set target dates and take steps towards
   self-government and independence by 1965;

c. help formulate and finance policies of economic,
   educational, and political development for the
   people of Portuguese Africa to prepare them for an
   independence with responsibility.

He did not hesitate to be critical of the policies of the U.S.
government on southern Africa. He said in the memo:

In order to achieve these ends the United States should
not depend solely upon "quiet diplomacy," but should
from time to time make positive suggestions of courses

of action which she believes to be right. It is imperative that the United States take a strong exception to the massacre of Angolans which even the most conservative newspapers report as taking place everyday. If the United States was justified in publicly condemning the South African Government for the Sharpeville massacre, where less than one hundred people were killed, it should be even more horrified by the thousands of Africans who are being butchered by the Portuguese army in Angola. Furthermore, the United States of America could set aside funds for the education of Africans from Portuguese Africa, in order to prepare them for their forthcoming independence. For this purpose it could establish an organization through which it could carry out a carefully planned programme of education. The United States Government need not depend on the co-operation of the Portuguese Government, but seek every means possible to implement that programme.

Notwithstanding Eduardo's doubts about the ability to influence the Portuguese government, Tom proceeded with his plans for the ecumenical press conference at the National Council of Churches on June 9. Two months later, Tom recognized that the goal of influencing the government of Portugal to begin the process of discussing with African leaders the change to independence was not successful.

The summer of 1961 was when Tom visited Africa to meet with African leaders so he could include them in his book. Friends in the Department of State discouraged him from

Eduardo Mondlane, martyr for Mozambican independence.

attempting to visit either Angola or Mozambique, as they believed that the press conference on the open letter to the government of Portugal in June 1961 resulted in Tom having a negative file with the Portuguese police. Consequently he did not visit Angola or Mozambique, but kept up the contacts with Holden Roberto and Eduardo Mondlane in the United States. Tom told Margaret later that he saw Eduardo Mondlane as a person moved by idealism, but who still recognized political realities. The reality was that the government of Portugal was not ready to participate with Africans in the process of political change in their African colonies.

When we received word on February 3, 1969, that Eduardo had been killed at his office in Dar es Salaam, Tom said to Margaret that Eduardo was correct in his analysis. He was killed by a bomb that was sent through the mail in a box indicating that it was a book. In opening the package he was killed, and thus became a martyr to the cause of Mozambican independence.

In the memo that Eduardo sent to Tom, he pointed out that the Portuguese government was administering Mozambique with a policy that was "a combination of political oppression, lack of educational facilities, and economic subservience that made it almost impossible for the African to progress in the Mozambique social structures." Eduardo was accurate in his analysis.

For us, Eduardo Mondlane was in some ways a "new face" on the African liberation circuit. With the exception of Holden Roberto and Seretse Khama, the other leaders (Senghor of Senegal, Nyerere of Tanzania, Tom Mboya of Kenya) were Catholic and benefited from those connections. Kaunda, the son of a Presbyterian minister, remained Protestant but clearly benefited in his early days from his Irish Catholic connections. However Mondlane, like the other African leaders, had a very good sense of ecumenical cooperation. We put him in contact with Catholic Relief Services, and we immediately heard in 1961 and 1962 about his request for medical and clothing assistance for the Mozambique refugees who were living primarily in Tanzania and Zambia.

Early Life

When Eduardo Mondlane was born on June 20, 1920, little consideration was being given then to the thought that forty years later, in 1960, there would be a sweep of independence bringing with it most of the African colonies to the point of independence. As some would say, destiny arranged to have Eduardo born in a part of East Africa that was a colonial territory of Portugal. As in Anglola, Catholicism was an integral part of the Portuguese influence on the local culture of Mozambique. Yet, similar to Angola, Protestant missionaries played an important role in the education of future African leaders. Eduardo, at the young age of ten, met Swiss Presbyterian missionaries and attended their elementary school. He was simultaneously the son of a tribal chief and a charismatic young man. As with Senghor and Nyerere, his leadership potential, ambition, and commitment attracted the attention of European and American missionaries.

In the case of Eduardo, it was Protestant missionaries who nominated him to the Phelps-Stokes Fund in New York for a scholarship to study in the United States. Eduardo hesitated and selected the University in Portugal in Lisbon in the hopes that with an improved knowledge of Portuguese culture, he could help influence the direction of Portugal in regard to the African colonies. However, after a year of difficulties, including being harassed by Portuguese security services, Eduardo asked the Phelps-Stokes Fund to transfer his scholarship to an American institution. Thus, Eduardo attended Oberlin College, and in 1953 earned the B.A. degree. He immediately enrolled at Northwestern University, where he received the M.A. degree. He later earned a Ph.D. in anthropology from Harvard University.

Once he entered the professional world of academia and government, he rose rapidly in a succession of higher positions. Among the leaders of African independence in the 1960s, only Eduardo Mondlane and Léopold Senghor had earned doctorate degrees.

A very important part of his early life was his marriage to Janet Rae. While still a graduate student, he met Janet at a Christian summer camp. She is a white Protestant American, and it is reported that her parents were originally opposed to the marriage. However, when the sad funeral services were held for Eduardo, most agreed that she played a key role in the activities for the independence of Mozambique. When Mozambique finally obtained its independence in 1975, the memory of Eduardo Mondlane, who was killed six years earlier, in 1969, was very present.

The 1960s

Eduardo remained in contact with the Meladys through his various trips to New York. One of the first contacts we made for Eduardo was with Catholic Relief Services. On December 12, 1966, writing to us from Dar es Salaam, Eduardo was concerned that the medications that arrived from Catholic Relief Services would only meet a small percentage of the needs of the Mozambique refugees in the camps in Tanzania and Zambia. This was always a problem, as the medicines needed were generally for infectious diseases, and there was always a high demand for them. We then contacted both Church World Service and Lutheran World Relief, and they were able to supply additional medicines. Catholic Relief Services also supplied needed secondhand clothing for Mozambique refugee camps, as it did with the Angolans.

The clothing came from an annual collection at Thanksgiving time. Tons of clothing were gathered, sorted out, cleaned, and made available to thousands of people in need. We regretted that the church leadership ceased having the annual collection.

The pressing need always was for medical supplies. The situation for refugees in camps with a minimum of sanitation facilities inevitably caused diseases that could be disastrous. In 1965 we appealed to Catholic Relief Services, the National Council of Churches, and Lutheran World Relief for a cash contribution, which would allow Dr. Mondlane to buy the medical supplies in Dar es Salaam, where he was headquartered. We were pleased when he wrote to Tom on August 6 indicating that funds had been authorized for the medicine fund. We were even more pleased to note that it was an ecumenical response to a human need. This was clearly a positive factor in the leadership of Mondlane. He inspired ecumenical cooperation and support.

In the summer of 1962, we briefly visited the capitals of both Mozambique and Angola. Because we knew we were being watched by Portuguese officials, we conducted ourselves as tourists, simply seeing the cities and observing life in these colonies. Despite Portuguese resistance to preparing for independence, we noticed the intermingling of races — white, brown, and black. This was also evident in Mondlane's political operations. He asked Mozambicans of European and Asian descent to work together with Africans at the highest levels of his organization. We noticed too that Mondlane attracted people of all faiths — Christians, Moslems, Hindus and those of no faith — and invited them to join the effort. Mondlane made clear that the Mozambican struggle was not based on race.

The Catholic Problem in Mozambique

We were able to have candid discussions with Eduardo on the public relations problem for the Catholic Church among Mozambican refugees living in camps in Tanzania and Zambia. Tom soon recognized that Mondlane wanted to help the church resolve the problem of the appearance of support for the Portuguese military activities against the Mozambique liberation fighters campaigning for independence.

Tom had several meetings with Monsignor Alberto Giovanetti, Permanent Observer of the Holy See to the United Nations, in 1966. He arranged for Eduardo to submit a memo on the matter to Monsignor Giovanetti on February 7, 1967. It remained a sensitive matter, for in the minds of the average Mozambique resident it was difficult to separate the Catholic background of Portugal from the oppressive actions of the Portuguese government in Mozambique.

We believed that many from Mozambique could resent the Catholic Church because of their negative view of the Portuguese military operations. Bishop Swanstrom of Catholic Relief

Services understood this as well as Eduardo Mondlane, a Protestant layman. Since it took fifteen years of struggle after the sweep of freedom occurred in black Africa in 1960, there was a period of severe dislike for the Catholic position. We appreciated Mondlane's wish in the preparation of the people of Mozambique for independence to reduce this bias. He did not live to witness the results of his ecumenical humanism, but there is no question that he moved the country in the right direction.

The Mozambique Institute

Eduardo Mondlane, with the assistance of his wife, founded the Mozambique Institute. They thought of the future and wanted to prepare young people for their future in an independent country. The Institute received an initial grant from the Ford Foundation, but it was not renewed because the Foundation noted the political involvement of the Institute with the independence movement.

Mondlane was, in some ways, an easy person to assist. An example of this was in 1965 when Tom was contacted by Henry Leir, a New York business leader and philanthropist who wanted to meet the leader from Mozambique. After the meeting Henry Leir sent a contribution restricted to aiding the Mozambique refugees.

Eduardo Mondlane's strong dedication to providing education to the Mozambique people was part of his attractiveness. He was a revolutionary leader with a Ph.D.

On two occasions Eduardo asked us to host a reception for Mozambique petitioners who would come for the U.N.

General Assembly session. We were pleased to do this and put a heavy emphasis on inviting representatives of the various refugee assistance groups and labor organizations. The efforts of Dr. Mondlane to present the face and facts of Mozambique were always carried out on a "shoestring" budget. It was basically a matter of getting those who believed in the goal of freedom and independence to contribute accordingly to their ability.

After Mozambique had been a Portuguese colony for almost five centuries, it was always a pleasure to observe the Mozambicans taste the waters of independence, which for Mozambique would be in 1975.

We noted that Mondlane always took advantage of an opportunity to heal the problems for Catholics in Mozambique. In 1967 he approached us to assist in the visit of a Mozambican priest who as an underground worker had just escaped to Dar es Salaam. We understood that the appearance of a Mozambican priest supporting the independence cause would serve several good purposes.

The Students from Mozambique

The Department of State had an excellent program for students from southern Africa. A number of Mozambicans came to the United States under this program in the 1960s. We were approached by several of the students to assist in resolving a delicate matter. The coordinator of the U.S. government-sponsored program was placing some of them in a university that was attended primarily by African American students.

A delegation of three came to see Tom at the Africa Service Institute in New York City. They were sensitive on the matter, but told Tom that they wanted to have a multiracial experience in the United States. Why, they asked, were they being placed in schools overwhelmingly of African Americans? They furthermore claimed that their preference for attending a Catholic-related university in the United States was ignored.

Tom looked into the matter and verified that the administrators of the program at the Department of State were people of good will. There was no bias in their selection. It was a matter of facilitating the adjustment of the culture of the Mozambicans to that of the United States.

We were able to arrange some transfers of these students to Manhattan College and Fordham University. Many of the graduates of the southern African scholarship program have returned to their countries and are participating in the life of independent countries. This includes a nucleus of students recommended by Eduardo for educational programs in the United States. They are now serving in the independent state of Mozambique.

Eduardo Mondlane: Martyr

A very dear friend and supporter of African independence, Shirley Smith, phoned us on February 3, 1969, with the sad news that Eduardo Mondlane was assassinated in Dar es Salaam, Tanzania. He was dead at forty-nine. A bomb had been placed inside a book that was sent to him. There was never a full investigation about who was responsible. At the time of his murder some blamed Portuguese secret police, others accused disgruntled members of the Mozambique liberation movement, but no one disputed his legacy. Eduardo's classmate from Oberlin, Rev. Edward Hawley, summarized his life in a few words; "Mondlane laid down his life for the truth that man was made for dignity and self determination."

After Shirley's phone call, we reflected on our last meeting with Eduardo at his headquarters in Dar es Salaam. He embraced us on arrival and was optimistic about the outcome: the people of Mozambique would be joining their brothers and sisters in the African countries that were now independent. He had an infectious charm; his smile always came easily and was so totally natural. In looking back on our last visit, we recalled that the building where he was headquartered had only young enthusiastic supporters. Where was the security?

It was the end for Eduardo. We would add several words to the remarks of Rev. Hawley. He was also a man who cared for people. He was a man of reconciliation.

Works by and about
Eduardo C. Mondlane

Mondlane, Eduardo. *The Struggle for Mozambique*. Harmondsworth: Penguin Books, 1969.

Henriksen, Thomas H. *Eduardo C. Mondlane: His Political Philosophy*. African Studies Association, 1971

Kitchen, Helen. "Conversations with Eduardo Mondlane." *Africa Report* no. 2 (November 1967): 51.

Maxwell, Kenneth. *The Making of Portuguese Democracy*. Cambridge: Cambridge University Press, 1995.

Chapter Eight

WILLIAM V. S. TUBMAN
New Deal for Liberia

Tom's first experience in Africa was in Ethiopia. He was there on his first overseas assignment with the Foreign Operations Administration (now known as the Agency for International Development). In preparing for the assignment, he knew there were two countries in sub-Saharan Africa that were independent and that had a long history of independence at the time of his trip in 1955. They were Ethiopia and Liberia.

In moving to and living in Ethiopia, Tom could feel the pride of the Ethiopians. An ancient kingdom, they were the only African state to defeat one of the European colonial powers in the nineteenth century. In the scramble for colonies in Africa, in 1896 Emperor Menelik the Great defeated the Italian army at the battle of Adowa. While Ethiopia was occupied by Mussolini's troops from 1936 to 1941, Emperor Haile Selassie left the country but never abdicated. And furthermore, he led allied and Ethiopian troops in one of the first victories against the Axis powers in World War II when Ethiopia was freed from an oppressive Fascist occupation.

Liberia, on the west coast of Africa, had an entirely different history. In 1816, a group of philanthropists and Protestant

Church leaders in the northern states of the United States launched the American Colonization Society. At that time in the United States, there were around 2 million black slaves and around 200,000 African American "free men." The goal of the American Colonization Society was to relocate the freed slaves to Africa — the homeland of their ancestors. On July 26, 1847, the settlers declared Liberia to be a sovereign independent state.

Although founded with the idealism of resettling freed slaves in the continent of their ancestors, the newly established country of Liberia faced many problems and tribulations from the very beginning.

When Tom made his first trip to West Africa in 1960, he was shocked by the negative remarks of both black and white leaders in Africa about Liberia. Whether the negative remarks were said with a French accent or the English accent of leaders in Ghana, it was one of sarcasm and derision for the "poor and struggling" Liberia.

Tom, perplexed by the jokes about Liberians that he heard from other Africanists, decided to spend a few days in Monrovia on his 1960 trip. He met with William V. S. Tubman and decided that Tubman was not to be laughed at, that within the history and culture of Liberia, he could be the greatest leader. All our subsequent visits to Liberia confirmed Tom's original estimation of Tubman.

On the same 1960 visit, in a conversation with Léopold Sédar Senghor, the poet-philosopher-intellectual founding president of Senegal, the name of Tubman came into the conversation. President Senghor said that he saw Tubman as a true revolutionary. He emphasized his practicality in meeting the challenges

Lawrence Marinelli chatting with President Tubman about Marinelli's book *The New Liberia* in 1963. Source: *The New Liberia:* Praeger

of Liberia. Senghor, in a 1964 article, said, "We do not smile at Liberia the way we did before 1944." In his lifetime, he has entered into the history of the continent; never will he leave it.

We had great respect for the observations of Senghor. We felt strongly that Liberia had an inherent cultural challenge not facing the other countries. As Tubman moved upward rapidly in the 1960s, we could never verify if he was aware of the statement in 1817 by the "Free Negroes in Philadelphia" to their representative in Congress, Joseph Hopkinson: "To thrust the free people of color into the wilds of Africa without a knowledge of the arts and sciences and without a government of any kind is to send them into perpetual bondage." In our opinion they correctly predicted the cultural confusion and impotence that would occur.

While well-meaning church leaders took the lead in assisting in the settlement of former slaves in Liberia, the U.S. government observed the struggling new state with little interest. One reason was that in the nineteenth and early twentieth centuries of the United States, it would have been very difficult to obtain congressional approval for any assistance program.

Tubman, unlike most of the African leaders who participated in the 1960 sweep of independence, did not become the elected leader until he was an older man; in the case of Tubman, he was sixty-four. Born in 1895, he was one of the very few African leaders born in the nineteenth century. He knew from his six decades of living in Liberia that the number one challenge was to unite two societies into one state.

Who was the man who, in a later stage of his life, took on the challenge to bridge the enormous cultural gap between the less than 20,000 Americo-Liberians and the more than 1 million native Liberians? He did it alone. Unlike Senghor and Nyerere, he did not have powerful friends in Europe or the United States.

William Vacanarat Shadrach Tubman: Early Life

Tubman was the son of a clergyman, Reverend Alexander Tubman, and Elizabeth Tubman. He was born into the class of Americo-Liberians, descendants of former American slaves, who in the wake of the Protestant movement to assist freed African Americans to return to Africa arrived on the political scene in Liberia.

His clergyman father was also a leader in the group of less than 20,000 Americo-Liberians who essentially controlled the country until very recent years. The Americo-Liberian culture of that period had no strong factors calling for change like the African leadership circles in Senegal, Ghana, Kenya, and Zambia.

Liberia also bore the burden of its identification with the pre-nineteenth-century culture of the United States. Freed American slaves and their descendants settled on the west coast of Africa. They came from the fractured culture of the black family in the United States. Those who remained in the United States were part of the ever-improving quality of life and expectations for the African American family in the United States. For the freed American slaves and their descendants who returned to Liberia, it was a complex cultural experience, as most of their ancestors did not originate from Liberia. It is now believed that the majority of their ancestors came from central Africa, and many of the Americo-Liberians had transmitted to them by their slave parents or grandparents the folktales of another culture. Liberia, for more than a hundred years, was a country of "better connected" Americo-Liberians living on the coast, enjoying at a minimum level the benefits of American civilization. They were a distinct minority, who in most cases did not speak the language of the majority Vai, Kru, and Mande-Fu communities.

Tubman, who had made one visit in 1928 to the United States on behalf of his church, could easily see the challenge. It was almost herculean: a small minority who felt that destiny gave them certain privileges. It was also a difficult existence on the west coast of Africa. Most of the energies were spent in preserving their own interests. They had little time for their overwhelmingly illiterate neighbors in the hinterland. William V. S. Tubman saw the challenge and devoted his presidency of twenty-six years to significantly improve the life of all Liberians.

First Contacts with President Tubman

When Tom discussed his plans for meetings with African leaders on his 1961 visit to Africa, he noted that the small, articulate groups of American academics did not have Tubman high on their list of future influential leaders. Tom was not prepared to accept their downgrading of William V. S. Tubman after studying how he faced with determination and courage the problem of the cultural divide in Liberia. Tubman saw the seriousness of a two-society country and took drastic steps to significantly reduce the gap. Tom was aware of the double burden of Tubman: domestic and international. He believed that he was dedicated to resolving the domestic challenge.

Tom then wanted to test the waters on how Tubman viewed pressing African issues of the 1960s, and he sent a letter on May 5, 1961, to President Tubman asking for an appointment and also urging him to take up the cause of the Portuguese colonies in Africa. President Tubman responded in seven days and wrote to Tom as follows,

Your letter of May the 5th which you express deep concern for the repressive activities in Angola and other areas has been received.

The cause of the dependent nations of Africa and the rest of the world disturbs all nationalists. We in Africa are particularly disturbed over the recent atrocious events which, despite the transformations which have taken place on the Continent, still savour of man's inhumanity to man and the determination of certain diehards to keep others in subjection in the interest of their own selfish ends.

But events of the times and world sentiment continue to agitate the consciences of men of goodwill. Thus at the recent Monrovia Conference before Mr. Holden Roberto addressed the Conference, the body had already pledged moral and technical support to the people of Angola in their fight for self-determination. After Mr. Roberto's speech, this decision received further affirmation. The cause of the people of Angola was presented eloquently and with great appeal.

The Conference of the Heads of African and Malagasy States ended yesterday on a note of great harmony and unanimity on all the issues discussed. The implementation phase of the Conference will continue in Dakar three months hence when technical experts will meet to consider educational, economic, cultural, scientific, and technical cooperation as well as plans for communications and transportation among African and Malagasy States.

Those African leaders who continue to press for the true peace and prosperity of their nations and consequently the entire Continent of Africa can now look to the future with a greater optimism than ever before. It is my earnest wish that the peoples of the world of goodwill will take up the cause of African freedom and independence in a greater measure and thus help advance the cause which we all have so much at heart.

It will be a pleasure to see you in Monrovia and will look forward to reading your book *The Peoples of Africa* when it comes off the press.

The 1961 visit and contacts gave Tom a perceptive view of Tubman the man. His several days in Monrovia, which was one of the most unattractive cities on the African west coast, convinced Tom that the lack of appreciation for Tubman's leadership role was the erroneous perception that he was a local black political hack. Thus, the perception was that he was not a key player in the 1960s sweep of independence in sub-Saharan Africa.

The 1961 visit was also related to an awkward moment for Tom. In the lively discussion that he had with President Tubman, Tom suggested that the president consider on his next state visit to the United States an academic convocation where, honored with an honorary doctorate, he could give a major comprehensive address on the future of Africa. This he believed would give Tubman a dignified platform for presenting his views on African independence.

President Tubman, in his letter of August 15, 1961, said to Tom, "It will certainly be a gracious gesture of the Africa Service Institute to arrange for me to receive an honorary doctor of laws degree when next I visit the United States. I shall regard this a great privilege to be thus honored."

Beginning with 1961 and through 1966, Tom's nomination of William V. S. Tubman for an honorary doctorate with a full academic convocation never resulted in a clear offer. The sad fact was that as other leaders emerged, like Senghor, Nyerere, Kaunda, Mboya, Roberto, and Mondlane, the image of Tubman was weak and pale in comparison.

Most of our academic contacts were with Catholic universities. Since Catholics were a very insignificant minority in Liberia and the country was closely identified with Protestant and Masonic traditions, we were not successful in obtaining for him a high academic honor. Before President Tubman died on July 23, 1971, countries and institutions began to recognize that he in his own way was a double hero. He faced with courage the destructive culture gap in his country and was a significant force in the African liberation movement that gained hurricane force in the 1960s.

He was a loyal friend of the United States. He was always available to be helpful to the United States during the difficult years of the Cold War. This brought him the dislike of the Communist world and the left-wing media. He knew who he was and never attempted to be someone else. Recognition of his leadership came late, but he is now acknowledged as a leading figure in the 1960s sweep of independence in black Africa.

Liberia: Strong Friend of the United States

One of the first places where Tubman was able to demonstrate the full commitment of Liberia to the African Freedom

Movement was at the United Nations. In December 1960, Liberia was elected to the Security Council of the United Nations. Its one-year membership, until December 31, 1961, coincided with the first months of the sweep of independence. They were also the months of the troubling challenges in Angola, Algeria, the Congo, and southern Africa. Furthermore during this critical period, long-time Liberian ambassador Nathan Barnes was the president of the Security Council during the period after the death of U.N. secretary general Dag Hammarskjöld. Liberian ambassador Barnes played a significant role in defeating the Soviet Union's plans for a "troika" to replace Hammarskjöld. It was Liberia that influenced the U.N. Security Council to focus on the Angolan problem. Holden Roberto was always lavish in his praise of the success in Tubman's "quarterbacking" the work of a Liberian delegation to the United Nations. Liberia was a key player in obtaining the cooperation of other states, especially the United Arab Republic, and putting the Angolan problem on the agenda.

In the spring of 1961 when we worked to obtain support for the Protestant-Catholic leadership appeal to the government of Portugal to begin the process of change in Angola and Mozambique, the Liberian mission to the United Nations, and its Embassy in Washington were exceptionally helpful. Dealing with the United Nations is always complicated, and Tubman took pains to assure that two of his top diplomats, Ms. Angie Brooks and J. Rudolph Grimes, took the lead.

Liberia guided through the General Assembly of the U.N. the following resolution:

1. The subjection of peoples to alien subjugation, domination and exploitation constitutes a denial of fundamental human rights, is contrary to the Charter of the United Nations and is an impediment to the promotion of world peace and co-operation.

2. All peoples have the right to self-determination; by virtue of that right they freely determine their political status and freely pursue their economic, social and cultural development.

3. Inadequacy of political, economic, social or educational preparedness should never serve as a pretext for delaying independence.

4. All armed action or repressive measures of all kinds directed against dependent peoples shall cease in order to enable them to exercise peacefully and freely their right to complete independence, and the integrity of their national territory shall be respected.

5. Immediate steps shall be taken, in Trust and Non-Self-Governing Territories or all other territories which have not yet attained independence, to transfer all powers to the peoples of those territories, without any conditions or reservations, in accordance with their freely expressed will and desire, without any distinction as to race, creed or color, in order to enable them to enjoy complete independence and freedom.

6. Any attempt aimed at the partial or total disruption of the national unity and the territorial integrity of a country

is incompatible with the purposes and principles of the Charter of the United Nations.

7. All States shall observe faithfully and strictly the provisions of the Charter of the United Nations, the Universal Declaration of Human Rights and the present Declaration on the basis of equality, non-interference in the internal affairs of all States, and respect for the sovereign rights of all peoples and their territorial integrity.

These and other activities of the Liberian mission combined with the growing pressure from the humanitarian and religious organizations were part of the buildup to influence Portugal to change its policy. The buildup continued, and on September 27 Liberia's secretary of state addressed the General Assembly on the Angolan problem.

The Portuguese Government defiantly refused to permit the United Nations Commission to enter Angola to make the necessary inquiry.... I do not think it is necessary to go into the details of whether the territory is indeed a province of Portugal or not, for the overwhelming majority of the members of the United Nations wisely rejected that contention. Until August 28, 1961, in the so-called "province of Angola," with a population of four and a half million Africans, only about 30,000 have been assimilated and this after five hundred years of Portuguese civilization. But the announcement of August 28 by the Portuguese Minister of Overseas Provinces that the Angolans were then full citizens of Portugal and "are subject to a law which is the same for everyone, with no distinction of race, religion, or culture" is in our opinion an admission that nothing other than a repressive colonial regime continues to exist in that territory.

A dangerous practice seems to be developing on the part of some countries to ignore discussions taken by this organization and we have to be careful not to tolerate or permit it to go unchallenged. It is hoped that the Commission will make a full report.

Liberian Secretary of State Grimes continued building up the pressure on Portugal, and in September 1962 at the General Assembly declared,

My Government will...join in any reasonable action designed to persuade and coerce Portugal to see the error of its ways and to conform to the principles of the Charter. I desire to emphasize, however, that continued defiance of United Nations decisions is not compatible with membership in the United Nations.

President Tubman encouraged this strong and effective position of Liberia. After their efforts on Angola, Liberia turned its attention to other problems in southern Africa. Tubman saw the danger that Southwest Africa, through clever manipulation, could be incorporated into the Union of South Africa. He understood also the danger of South Africa, then practicing apartheid, gaining de facto control of what within a few years became the Republic of Namibia, free of legalized racism.

Thanks to Tubman's farsighted direction, Liberia played a significant role in assuring that the peoples of then Southwest Africa did not fall victim to the racist policies of South Africa.

Liberia had two neighbors, Ghana and Guinea. With the leadership of Kwame Nkrumah and Sékou Touré they were not always stable and predictable. By 1963, Tubman's image among the African leaders had risen considerably. They appreciated his understanding of strategy and tactics. Unfortunately, the new, more favorable image of Tubman held by African leaders did not pass over to many of the American Africanists.

It is understandable that in the past there were mixed reviews about Tubman's role in the initiation of Africa's sweep of independence in 1960. He was, for some, too close to the American governmental and business interests. For others he could not escape the cloud of being an Americo-Liberian.

In the funeral orations preceding his burial in Liberia in 1971, there was still only incomplete recognition of the role he played in both the development of his own country and in the sweep of independence in black Africa in the 1960s. As the mourners said goodbye to the man who served as their president for twenty-seven years, there was still not a full appreciation for the quality of leadership that peacefully transformed a weak West African republic to a more influential state that became a player in African affairs.

Nine years later, on April 12, 1980, a military coup overthrew the government headed by William R. Tolbert Jr., who had succeeded Tubman. The country was then overtaken by chaos, which lasted for almost two decades.

The aftershocks in the post-Tubman era are causing some observers of the African scene to again postpone their evaluation of William V. S. Tubman. We believe that an evaluation can now be made. Given all the special and exceptional circumstances in Liberia since its founding, we believe that in the long term he will be known as a leader who launched a new deal for Liberia. As President Senghor said about President Tubman, "In his lifetime, he has entered into the history of the continent, never will he leave it."

Books about
William V. S. Tubman

Bank Henries, A. Doris. *A Biography of President William V. S. Tubman.* London: Macmillan, 1968.

Dunn, D. E. *The Foreign Policy of Liberia during the Tubman Era, 1944–1971.* London: Hutchinson Benham, 1979.

Marinelli, Lawrence. *The New Liberia: A Historical and Political Survey.* New York: Praeger, 1964.

Smith, Robert A. *William V. S. Tubman: The Life and Work of an African Statesman.* Amsterdam: Van Ditmar, 1967.

Townsend, E. R., ed., *President Tubman of Liberia Speaks.* London: Consolidated Company, 1959.

Wreh, Tuan. *The Love of Liberty: The Rule of President William V. S. Tubman in Liberia, 1944–1971.* London: C. Hurst, 1976.

Chapter Nine

SYLVANUS OLYMPIO
Brutally Murdered in Togo

Within a few weeks of Tom being active in New York-U.N. circles in 1959, he heard a name that was frequently mentioned when the conversation focused on African leaders: Sylvanus Olympio. Starting in the early 1950s, he was at the United Nations at least once a year. The articulate university graduate came to the U.N. to set forth the initial process of seeking independence for Togo. In the process of doing that, he emerged as a popular West African leader.

Togo, a relic of the nineteenth-century colonial period, was a former German colony. Following World War I, it became a League of Nations mandate territory that was transferred to the United Nations in 1946.

Sylvanus Olympio, a London School of Economics graduate, set a high standard for petitioners visiting the United Nations. He was the symbol of engagement. He knew what he wanted: freedom, dignity, and independence for the black African people. He rejected the advocates of confrontation. A product of Western culture, he decided as a young leader that he would engage European and U.N. leaders in a dialogue on how to carry out the ideals of the trusteeship policy.

One of the amazing surprises of the Versailles Peace Treaty of 1919 was the trustee territory provision adopted by first the League of Nations in regard to the former colonies and later accepted by the United Nations.

> to promote the political, economic, social, and educational advancement of the inhabitants of the trust territories, and their progressive development towards self-government or independence as may be appropriate to the particular circumstances of each territory and its peoples and the freely expressed wishes of the peoples concerned, and as may be provided by the terms of each trusteeship agreement.

The historical record of centuries was for the winning power in a war to acquire some of the territory of the defeated power. That did not happen with the German colonies. The German colonies of Togo, Cameroon, German Southwest Africa, Tanganyika, and Rwanda-Burundi became the responsibility of the League of Nations in 1919. Togo was assigned to France, which had the administrative authority over most of the country. This unprecedented departure from the tradition of transferring one colony to the full control of another power was not continued in the case of the German colonies in Africa. This amazing new development in international affairs attracted little notice. However, the young man in the 1950s who understood the difference was Sylvanus Olympio. He understood the difference between a colony and a United Nations trustee territory. He also had a sense that the world was at the eve of significant change in regard to the third world. He, the product of the Western educational system, quickly concluded that the way to obtain independence for the trustee territories was to campaign on the theme that the African people are now ready.

Walking the halls of the U.N. and knocking at the doors of the various European and American embassies to the United Nations, he charmed both the U.N. authorities and the Western diplomats in all of these contacts. Olympio made his first visit to the U.N. Trusteeship Council in 1947. He pleaded each year before the Trusteeship Council on behalf of the Togolese people until independence was granted in 1960. There was never a confrontation; he was the personification of the art of engagement.

By the end of the 1950s, this made him the "big man" from Togo. Olympio, however, also understood the challenge that European colonialism had left for the people of West Africa. Tom remembers a conversation with him in the delegates' lounge of the U.N. Olympio focused on his role as a petitioner to establish that the people of Togo were now ready to proceed to the next level, which was independence.

Tom recalls leaving that first meeting with him overwhelmed that a man of such talent should now be able to walk the halls of the United Nations. In his hour and a half talk with Tom, Olympio never once criticized the colonial powers. He rather devoted most of the time to stating various facts that, in his opinion, should advance Togo to the stage of being considered for independence. He argued in terms of the U.N. Trusteeship Agreement and in more general terms of social justice. Tom made a mental note after the first meeting to research something about Olympio's background.

A Positive Presence

His grandparents had emigrated from Brazil, and soon evolved into an influential family in Lomé. A comfortable home background made it possible for him to attend first a German mission school and then local schools in the French part of the U.N. trusteeship territory of Togo. As a teenager he was fluent in German and French. His parents selected the London School of Economics for him, and he graduated in 1926 with a major in business. His competence, language abilities, and clear leadership abilities made him an attractive candidate for employment.

Sylvanus Olympio took a position with the Unilever Company, working first in Nigeria and later in the Ivory Coast. In 1929, he became assistant to the general manager of Unilever in Togoland. After nine years he was appointed general manager of the United Africa Company, a Unilever subsidiary.

Several years after the start of World War II, Olympio became a vice president of the Comité de l'Unité Togolaise (CUT). Some say he was its founder, but he himself generously awards this distinction to the French Governor Montagne, who started it as "purely and simply a cultural organization, as innocuous as one would expect an organization founded in the somber war days to be."

With the rapid evolution of Togoland since World War II, he became a leader in political affairs. He was a member of the Representative Assembly of Togo from 1946 to 1951 and then became a member of the Territorial Assembly of Togoland from 1952 to 1955.

By this time he was one of the acknowledged leaders of his country. With the setting up of the United Nations he became a regular visitor to New York in the interests of Togolaise independence. In 1956 the territory became an autonomous republic within the French community with a cabinet headed by Nicolas Grunitzky. The CUT abstained from the election, which was marked by various charges. A new election, with U.N. observers present, was held in 1958, and Olympio's CUT won thirty-six seats out of forty-six in the unicameral legislature.

Togo lies only a little north of the intersection of the equator and 0 degrees longitude, and is bounded by Ghana on the west and Benin (formerly Dahomey) on the east. Volta is to the north and the Atlantic is on the south. Its principal exports are coffee, 45 percent, and cocoa, 30 percent. Despite price troubles, the country was able to double its coffee production during 1959 (perhaps under the stimulus of independence) to 11,500 tons. Cocoa production also rose, to 8,000 tons.

In his main policy speech in May 1958, Olympio outlined his objectives for a new African state. In contrast to some lands where the authority of the tribal chiefs was regarded as being synonymous with backwardness, Olympio's party stated its intention to preserve chieftaincy as the "guarantee of our traditions" and as characteristic of those roots and traditions that "all societies however rapidly and dynamically evolving must always have." Reversing the trend that has been a problem of many more "highly developed" nations, Olympio decentralized government. Certainly there was no sounder way to develop the ability of a nation to govern itself than to place executive power in the hands of local councils. Olympio noted that this was the "first time in black Africa" that this had been done. The move toward local self-government was accompanied by encouragement of various "self-help" projects.

The Olympio government also stressed clean government and "an end to all direct or indirect corruption." It guaranteed total freedom of speech, movement, and assembly. In one of his famous statements he said, "We are not afraid of criticism, positive or negative, for public opinion is sacred." This was one of his famous statements.

The second visit occurred several weeks later when Tom, this time without an appointment, bumped into him leaving the delegates' lounge of the U.N. They talked again, and Tom noted that Sylvanus was thoroughly acquainted with all of the provisions of the United Nations Trusteeship Council. He also knew all the rights of the petitioner. They discussed educational systems, and Olympio pointed out to Tom the strengths and weaknesses of the French and English systems. He had a very positive style and would avoid making negative comments. Tom concluded that this was a man who would have a future in Africa.

Toward Full Independence

In doing further research on Olympio after his first meeting, Tom observed a similarity of Olympio with Senghor of Senegal. They both saw the positive elements of European civilization and looked for ways that the African peoples could benefit from continuing their association with the Europeans while at the same time obtaining their independence.

Togo was moving quickly toward its goal. In 1956 limited self-rule was granted, and the Togo administration proceeded to organize for the 1958 elections. During this time, Olympio organized the Comité de L'Unité Togolaise. Being a member of the Ewe tribe, Olympio through the party (CUT) campaigned for Ewe reunification, as members of the tribe were located not only in Togo, but also in Ghana and Dahomey (now Benin). Olympio made a strong point also of proposing stronger links between Togo and France. In the post–World War II period, he was active in Togolese programs, but always remained in contact with French government circles.

When French Togo received limited autonomy in 1956, the speed of moving toward full independence was accelerated. Olympio served as prime minister of Togo from 1958 to 1961. During this time, both his power and influence increased, and he became better known in African circles.

After Tom's two meetings with him in 1960, and a brief meeting in 1961, Tom placed him on the list of African leaders who would not only be influential in their home country, but who would be players in the unfolding drama of Africa moving quickly on the road to independence. He won early recognition in Washington. Olympio was the black African leader who spoke German, French, and English, as well as several African languages. The tall, engaging person who knew how to practice engagement was a well-known figure in New York–U.N. circles.

In preparing for our visit to Togo, Tom had written to Olympio saying that we would be visiting Lomé. He sent us a telegram assuring us of a warm welcome. We landed at the Ghana airport, where we had arranged for a driver to take us to Lomé, the capital of Togo. The following day, we were driven to President Olympio's residence. It was a beautiful clear day with a slight breeze coming in from the ocean. When we got there, Sylvanus Olympio, tall, handsome, and smiling, greeted us with a warm welcome. He said in a loud voice, "Come on up. Come on up." He embraced both of us, and we sat down and talked for an hour and a half.

It was 1962; the sweep of independence was in full progress. Olympio could see the early results in West Africa. Calm, cool, and relaxed, he discussed the issues. While recognizing that there would be many bumps in the road, he remained essentially optimistic. In regard to international affairs, he had no question about where Togo and the West African states should align their interests. In talking with us, we could see that he was obviously influenced by both a business education and his almost two decades of working in the business world. We both thought what a great friend of the United States and the West he would be. Olympio knew that he had responsibilities for his own people, and he talked pragmatically about an educational program that would encourage small business development. When elected president of the republic on April 9, 1961, he said, "Togo is prepared to work nonstop in order to raise up rapidly the social and economic standards of the country."

Olympio was full of optimism after his official visit with President Kennedy, who obviously believed that his administration was at the beginning of the sweep of independence in black Africa. Several of the African leaders Kennedy met when he was still a U.S. Senator in charge of the Senate Subcommittee on Africa had become heads of government. Sylvanus Olympio was among the African leaders that President Kennedy had met while a member of the U.S. Senate. An indication of Kennedy's strong belief, starting with his election in November 1960, that his administration would coincide with the historic developments taking place in Africa was that in the first two years of his administration, eleven African leaders were official visitors to the United States. President Sylvanus Olympio was the eleventh.

He arrived on March 20, and his two days in Washington were followed by three in New York. President Kennedy was profuse in his red-carpet welcome to President Olympio, saying that he was "an exceptional figure, not only in Africa, but on the world scene." President Olympio responded to the president's remarks with enthusiasm and, as he said, he looked forward to the visit "with almost boyish eagerness." Aware of the severe famine conditions in Northern Togo, President Kennedy announced in his meeting with President Olympio that the United States would make immediately available surplus food commodities for Togo and that furthermore Togo would benefit from the "Food for Peace" program that would assist in stimulating socioeconomic development in Togo.

Academic Recognition

His three days in New York City were always at a high level of positive excitement. We had recommended him to receive an honorary doctorate of laws at Fordham University, which responded quickly and affirmatively to the proposal. We were invited to be in the entourage that escorted the president to the

Sylvanus Olympio at Fordham University in 1962 with university president Father McGinley (l.) and Father John LaFarge, S.J. (r.), one of the
founders of the Catholic interracial movement.

Fordham University campus. Father Lawrence McGinley, university president, welcomed President Olympio to the ceremony
with these words of praise:

> It is a delightful occasion, indeed, when this university has
> the opportunity to bestow its highest academic honor upon
> a man of such varied talents, interests, and background. His
> Excellency has been a scholar, a successful businessman,
> a political theorist, and the leader of his people.
>
>   During the span of his life he has not only drawn deeply
> upon the rich traditions of his own nation and continent

but has also observed and tested the ideas and customs of many European nations and their broadly divergent attitudes. Beginning his education in a German mission school, he later studied in both English and French schools and, after the partitioning of Togo into British and French mandates, ultimately finished his studies in an English school. Finally, while studying politics and economics in the London School of Economics and Political Science, he undertook several study tours which brought him to France, Austria, Germany, Holland, and Italy. This is not his first visit either to this country on this city.

The breadth of his educational and cultural experience, then, has been great, and it is not excessive to say that His Excellency has made outstanding use of his opportunities. For out of these experiences has come not only his great personal success but also the wise leadership that he has given his newly independent nation in its hours of greatest challenge.

It is particularly interesting to note, I believe, that in the background of his cosmopolitan exposure to cultures, customs, ideals, and ideas has always been the inspiring figure of Holy Mother the Church, with her ancient philosophy of the common bond among all men by reason of their common origin and their common birth in Jesus Christ unto freedom as the Sons of God.

Olympio responded warmly and enthusiastically to the citation conferring on him the highest academic accolade. He spoke almost extemporaneously, looking only briefly at notes in his hand. He had studied at the London School of Economics, and he understood the recognition of the university's honorary doctorate. When he departed the campus on March 23 with his infectious smile, Margaret said to Tom what a blessing it was that the West African people had Sylvanus E. Olympio as a leader. We knew that he was the president of Togo, but as he faced the distinguished group at the convocation and spoke so firmly about the future, we too felt assured that with his strength and his voice there would be a firm advocate not only for independence, but also for reconciliation and understanding.

When we saw him in the summer of 1962, just several months after the academic convocation, he was still full of joy and optimism. When we said goodbye to Olympio after a very warm conversation, he responded with a hug. His last words to us were that he would see us soon at the U.N. We returned with joy in our hearts to the hotel, being thankful that such a great man was playing a lead role in the independence movement in West Africa. Little did we realize on that wonderful evening in Lomé that a few months later, on January 13, 1963, we would receive a phone call from friends in Washington advising us that he had been assassinated under peculiar circumstances in or near his home in Lomé.

Assassination

We had noticed that one of his strong principles was a devotion to a carefully balanced budget. This was a natural result of his longtime association with the Western business world. Unfortunately, he was different from many of his colleagues in the revolutionary movements of West Africa. They recalled the

days of colonialization and felt that they had a right to a government that would go into debt to take care of their needs.
Olympio had other ideas, and at the end of 1962, rumors were
reported that he was planning to balance the budget by cutting
some of the expenditures. He also believed that the military
budget, no longer being paid for by the French government, but
by the independent state of Togo, had to be reduced. A young
and small state, Togo did not have an internal intelligence system. There were no warnings for him on January 12, 1963, when
he retired at his home. A little past midnight, he was awakened
by a noise in the area that separated his residence from the U.S.
Embassy. It is unfortunate that in the killing of this pioneer in
the African liberation movement, there was never a respected
official investigation of all the circumstances, nor a report to the
world community. It is however believed that the report of the
daughter of the U.S. ambassador, Leon B. Poullada, is accurate.

President Olympio was killed in the early morning. He hid
from the ex-French army Togolese mercenary soldiers in a
car located in the United States Embassy car fleet. At that
time, the U.S. Embassy office was next to the President's
residence, sharing a wall in common. The U.S. ambassador
(my father) and the U.S. Deputy Chief of Mission (DCM)
(who is in his mid-nineties and had now provided details
of what is written here) were alerted in the middle of the
night, at about 3:30 a.m., that soldiers had gone into the
Embassy office property. My father went to the Embassy
office to find out what was going on, and to make sure

there was no damage to U.S. Embassy property and that all U.S. Embassy personnel were safe.

The ambassador's daughter went on to state,

> When my father returned with the DCM to the Embassy offices, shortly before 7:00 a.m., there were still soldiers in the area, and they found that a car door to one of the Embassy cars was open. President Olympio was lying on the ground by the gate, where he had been shot dead. He was dressed very informally and had no shoes on. Soldiers were in the street and were leaving. The DCM called the terrified (and unarmed) night watchman and they covered and moved President Olympio away from the Embassy office's gate. My father then contacted the Togolese archbishop and requested that he come take charge of President Olympio's remains safely and honorably. President Olympio's assassination was one of the worst and most devastating experiences of my father's years in the U.S. Foreign Service. My father not only deeply admired and even loved Olympio: he considered President Olympio to be one of his mentors in life. Throughout the remainder of my growing up, a very large black-framed photo portrait of President Olympio hung in the hall of our house, and it is hanging in the hall of my mother's house to this day. (See *www.reference.com/browse/Olympio.*)

It is regrettable that the distinguished life of Sylvanus Olympio ended in such a brutal fashion and that there was not a respected group that could formally investigate not only the immediate circumstances of the assassination, but of other factors leading up to it. Once we were advised of his assassination, we were active in various matters. We played an active role in organizing the appropriate memorial service for him, but before that could be done Tom was asked by the Department of State to be the one who would convey the sad news to his son Elpidio, who was a student at Princeton University. His older son, Gilchrist, a student at Hamilton College, had been notified directly by the U.S. government. The following day Tom called Cardinal Francis Spellman, archbishop of New York, about arranging a memorial service at the cathedral. He readily accepted, as he recalled Olympio had attended Mass at the cathedral when he was in the United States to see President Kennedy in May 1962.

The memorial Mass for President Olympio took place on February 13 at St. Patrick's Cathedral. U.S. Ambassador Adlai E. Stevenson, representative of President Kennedy at the Mass, more than two hundred U.N. diplomats, and other U.S. officials attended. We arranged for Elpidio Olympio to attend. We sat with him in the cathedral. As the more than a thousand people left the cathedral, there was a pall of sadness. There was no reception; most left quickly for their offices. We joined a few friends who, like us, were admirers of Sylvanus. This was the first assassination in this historic period of the sweep of independence. The details of the killing were confusing. The reports that this great friend and admirer of the United States was unable to gain admission to the safety of the Embassy compound were indeed very disturbing. It was a troubling time for

us attending the luncheon on Wednesday surrounded by others
running to their respective assignments.

In the months following Olympio's death we maintained contact with Elpidio, who was continuing his studies at Princeton.
During the Christmas season of 1963, Elpidio was especially
upset and sad that there was never a judicial procedure in
regard to the murder of his father. We suggested that he write
to the *New York Times.* He did and phoned to inform us that
a reporter from the newspaper was coming to the university to
interview him.

The *Times* reported his moving interview on January 26,
1964. The young man said, "I find it distressing that, up to
now, no commission of inquiry has been set up to investigate
such an unworthy act."

What the young Olympio said in 1964 remains true. It would
be probable that in today's world, with the experience of the
judicial procedures against leaders alleged to have committed
crimes in the former Yugoslavia and in Liberia, that a formal
inquiry would have been established.

We retained our original image of the strong, articulate West
African leader who wished to apply the lessons of engagement
in the development of his country. He was far ahead in thinking
and in experience of the disgruntled soldiers who, in the early
hours of January 13 killed him either at his home or in the U.S.
Embassy grounds. It was a sad moment for West Africa, as he
could have joined Senghor in giving enlightened leadership in
the early years of the sweep of independence in West Africa. We
never returned to visit Togo after the death of Sylvanus Olympio

because of the close association of the subsequent leaders of the country with the assassination.

Books by and about Sylvanus Olympio

Olympio, Sylvanus E. *Struggle for Africa South of the Sahara.* New York, 1953.

Hatch, John. *A History of Postwar Africa.* New York: Praeger, 1965.

Segal, Ronald. *Political Africa.* New York: Praeger, 1961.

Shachter Morgenthau, Ruth. *Political Parties in French Speaking West Africa.* Oxford: Clarendon Press, 1967.

Welch, Claude E., Jr. *Dream of Unity: Pan Africanism and Political Unification in West Africa.* Ithaca, N.Y.: Cornell University Press, 1966.

For an authoritative account of Olympio's murder see the Koffigoh Commission Report, 2005, and Livre Blanc, July 1963, the National Report on political events leading to President Olympio's death. See also "Death at the Gate." *Time,* January 25, 1963.

Chapter Ten

AHMADOU AHIDJO
Serene Leader of a Multiethnic Cameroon

In Tom's 1959–60 visits to Africa, he was always especially interested in meeting African leaders of the Islamic faith. There was no difficulty in meeting them. He saw and had conversations with Mokhtar Ould Daddah of Mauritania, Modibo Keita of Mali, Sékou Touré of Guinea, and Abubaka Tafawa Balewa of Nigeria. These gentlemen were from countries that were overwhelmingly Muslim. Tom was particularly interested in a Muslim leader in a country where there was a significant number of Christians. The ability to engage and guide multiethnic and pluralistic societies would, for Tom, be a sign of strong leadership.

He found this leader. He was Ahmadou Ahidjo of the Republic of the Cameroons. His record was impressive. Foreign states were responsible for one of the three major challenges he faced on January 1, 1960, when the country became independent and he became the first president of the republic. The Cameroon, a former German colony, was essentially divided in the mandate system between the French who had the northern area, and the British who had the southwest. This division brought two different styles of European administration and two different languages. This difference was also matched by the fact

152

that the northern part of the Cameroon was inhabited primarily by members of the Muslim faith and the south by Christians, mostly Catholic. Since the emerging independence of Cameroon took place during the Cold War, communist agitators regarded Cameroon as the most likely area in West Africa that could be taken over by a communist-dominated government.

The late 1950s and the first months of the 1960s were periods of riots and chaos. On his 1960 visit to Africa, when visiting Lomé, Tom was told by an Embassy staff officer that there were disturbances in Douala and that he would be well advised to avoid visiting the city at this time. Tom was disappointed because he wanted to see the situation for himself and to obtain a visit with President Ahidjo. The same problem existed for Tom in 1961, so he avoided Douala and went directly to Yaoundé, where President Ahidjo received him at his office with little advance notice. The interview was done in French, and Tom was impressed with the serenity of Ahidjo in view of the disruptive conditions in the major cities of the country. Ahidjo spoke openly about the problems, and with quiet determination assured Tom that the multiethnic country would remain unified.

He spoke clearly about the responsibilities of the state and seemed to understand, as far as Tom could detect, that the Cameroon would practice the ideals of pluralism. When Tom saw Ahidjo in July 1961, he was still the prime minister. It was a few months later on October 1, 1961, with the merger of the southern Cameroons, that the Federal Republic of Cameroon was established. Under this constitution Ahidjo became the federal president, and John M. Foncha of the southern Cameroon became vice president. On the same visit Tom was also able to see John Foncha, who was an enthusiastic supporter of a unified Cameroon.

Ahidjo faced the challenges of a multiethnic country by moving rapidly to establish subdivisions in the country that were not based primarily on ethnic or religious considerations. He divided the country into seven provinces. He initiated other changes that helped to unify Cameroon into a state. The railway system was expanded to connect the north and south portions of the country. He launched a road-building program that had the same goal in mind: unifying the various ethnic communities into one state.

Ahidjo, who did not benefit from university education, decentralized the university system (there was, when he initiated this action in 1962, only the University of Yaoundé). He was responsible for the other universities established in other areas of Cameroon.

Ahidjo was a determined leader who ruled using authoritarian methods, resulting in sometimes being called a dictator. However, in 1982, Ahidjo resigned for health reasons and facilitated the transfer of executive authority to the then prime minister Paul Biya, a Christian. Biya was also from the south. Ahidjo withstood heavy pressure to facilitate a transfer to another Muslim from the north. Ahidjo presented what he advocated: pluralism in a multiethnic state.

Ahidjo: The Background

Ahmadou Ahidjo was born in northern Cameroon in 1924. At that time, this part of the Cameroon was a French mandate territory. Ahidjo consequently grew up speaking French, as well as the several native languages. In terms of the local culture, he was born into a semiprivileged family. His father was a Fulani village chief. There was never any question about his religion. Ahidjo's mother raised him as a Muslim. Unlike the case of many of the other African leaders, the possibility of a university education was never discussed. But his family was interested in preparing him for contemporary society. Following elementary education, his family sent him to Yaoundé, where he was enrolled in the French secondary school. While a young student he had some of the characteristics of an adolescent athlete, as he played soccer and was a cyclist. While in secondary school, he became especially interested in radio and electronic communications, and in the beginning this was to be the direction of his career.

In 1942, while French administrators were busily involved in World War II, Ahidjo was admitted to the civil service and assigned to the postal system as a radio operator. It was this job that gave him the experience of visiting all the major cities of the Cameroon. As a Cameroonian from the north and a Muslim, he worked in the southern areas of the country, which were predominately Christian. It is believed that this pragmatic experience of working in the two different cultural-religious areas of the Cameroon, plus his easy contact with French and British administrators, gave this man a de facto experience of working with multiethnic communities without the higher education benefit of West African leaders like Senghor and Olympio. The end product was the same for all three, an appreciation for multiethnic and interreligious harmony. In the meetings of West African leaders, Ahidjo was always considered both as more conservative and less charismatic. In comparison to Senghor and Olympio, he was regarded as being less of an intellectual. There is now no question that he was one of the most influential leaders of West Africa.

These observations were made by people who understood the situation that faced him as a leader in the early 1960s in the Cameroon. There was disorder, bordering on chaos. There was also a religious divide, and the legacy of two European administrations. By the mid 1960s, however, Ahmadou Ahidjo had emerged as a leader of a country that survived these handicaps and that, in comparison with the other West African countries, was offering comparative prosperity.

These first few years of Cameroonian independence saw a quick transition of the structure of government. On January 1, 1960, French Cameroun was granted independence by France, with Ahmadou Ahidjo as president. On October 1, 1961, the formally British administered southern Cameroons united with the French Cameroun and formed the United Republic of Cameroon. By 1966, under the guidance of Ahidjo, the name of the republic became the Federal Republic of Cameroon. These were complicated political maneuvers, and Ahidjo turned out to be a very good quarterback.

While orchestrating these structural changes, Ahidjo, a pragmatist, also focused on the economy. He put an emphasis on cash crops and especially petroleum exploration. The oil money allowed the government to support farmers and to finance major development projects.

During this time the Republic of Cameroon with its stable leadership emerged as a powerful influence in African affairs.

U.S. Department of State

President Ahidjo with Undersecretary of State David Newsom in 1978.

Ahidjo, knowing the value of the United Nations for African states, maintained a very good delegation to the United Nations. It was during this time that we both believed that Ahmadou Ahidjo had not received the attention that his successful managing of Cameroonian affairs warranted.

He began his term as president with three handicaps. In our opinion he was ignored by leaders in the growing and influential community of American Africanists. Olympio, Mboya, and Kaunda seemed to attract more media attention. In Tom's 1965 visit to the Cameroon (Margaret stayed in Spain because we were expecting our first child) he discussed with Ahidjo steps that could be taken to obtain more media acknowledgment of the success of the Cameroon in the first decade of the sweep of independence.

Tom, while in Yaoundé, renewed his contact with Archbishop Zoa, the head of the Catholic Church in Cameroon, who was also Cameroonian. Tom's basic goal was to verify with the archbishop that the Muslim chief of state was not only speaking about pluralism, but also enacting rules and guidelines that both encourage and protect religious freedom. Archbishop Zoa endorsed the commitment of Ahidjo and testified to his success in establishing the framework for a pluralistic and multiethnic state.

University Accolades

After returning to the United States from his African trip, Tom also discussed the matter with Father Henry J. McAnulty, longtime president of Duquesne, who as a Spiritan priest was very sympathetic to African aspirations for independence, and he agreed that the university would convene a special academic convocation and confer an honorary doctorate on President Ahidjo. Spiritan missionaries had a long experience of working in Cameroon. Chiefs of state, even in accepting invitations from private institutions, must work out the details and obtain the support of the country's administration where they will visit. In this case there was no difficulty, but it took several months to work out the details. Tom discussed the matter with Joseph Palmer, then assistant secretary of state for African affairs. President Ahidjo told Tom, while visiting the United States, that he wished to have sufficient time to meet with and lobby at the United Nations in New York.

October 21, 1967, was selected as the mutually convenient date. The university, halfway into the fall semester, would stage a major convocation where a university affiliated with the Catholic Church would honor President Ahidjo, a Muslim. The university also wanted to give a major reception following the event. With all of the appropriate academic fanfare, the quiet and serene president of the Republic of Cameroon, with an established record of leadership of a multiethnic country, was praised with the following citation read by the president of the university:

Ahmadou Ahidjo, President of the Federal Republic of Cameroon, patriot —

We salute you as a man whose love of country is written into the history of a nation. As a youth you dedicated your life to the cause of the emancipation and reunification of your fatherland. From the beginning your chosen

weapons were negotiation and accommodation of differences — weapons of peace which you championed and
with which you worked tirelessly to build, step by step,
toward attainment of your goal.

When first independence, then reunification were won,
yours was to be the true reward of wise and dedicated
leadership: the challenge of a new cause. It was to you
that four million free citizens entrusted the highest office
and future course of their newborn nation. It is in you
that they continue to trust as you lead them in the peaceful building of the Federal Republic of Cameroon into a
unified, progressive and prosperous nation.

Duquesne is proud to heap her accolades on a man who,
in the span of a still-young lifetime, has earned the highest
tribute of his countrymen and the respect of the world.

The reception following the convocation was attended by
over two hundred invited guests, all of whom were personally
introduced to him. The guests included Archbishop Lefebvre,
then head of the Spiritan order throughout the world. Repre-
senting the United States government was Assistant Secretary
of State Joseph Palmer. Toward the end of the exciting reception, we had one little incident that needed to be tranquilized
before it marred the ceremonies. A city of Pittsburgh government bureaucrat asked us why the honorary doctorate was a
doctorate of economics and not of laws. Actually, Tom had
proposed to Father McAnulty that the university confer the
traditional honorary doctorate of doctorate of laws. We heard
for the first time the term doctorate of economics when the

citation was read at the ceremony. It was clear to us that the city functionary was inclined to make an issue of it. We were sensitive to the fact that the honoree was a black Muslim. It was necessary to immediately kill the possibility of a rumor that the university did not confer a "first class" honorary doctorate, but rather a "second class" honorary doctorate on the distinguished visitor because of his religious and racial background. For fifteen or twenty minutes we were both concerned. Tom pointed out to the inquisitive city official that a doctorate in economics related very closely to the actual accomplishment of President Ahidjo in stressing the economic development of his country. This one little incident we concealed from everyone else. At the end of the day we knew it was a most successful affair and accomplished what we wanted — putting the spotlight on Ahmadou Ahidjo, who led his country in the first years with courageous leadership. We could not help but note how carefully these events must be planned, especially where you have the participants of different racial and ethnic backgrounds. Furthermore, we noted that "small minds" will always find a negative element in an event that was full of good purposes.

The following morning Tom met with President Ahidjo at the hotel in Pittsburgh, where they were both residing. He was clearly appreciative of having received his first honorary doctorate from an American university. We remained in contact with President Ahidjo, following with interest his retirement from the presidential position for reasons of health in 1982. A year following his resignation he left Cameroon and went into exile in France.

The young Republic, like most in Africa in the 1960s and 1970s, had not yet worked out a retirement program for its former chiefs of state as the United States has done.

While in exile in France, Ahidjo was accused of participating in a conspiracy against the Cameroonian government. A death sentence was subsequently commuted. There remain many questions about the trial in Cameroon. After a year in France, Ahidjo moved to Dakar, Senegal, where he died in 1989.

Ahmadou Ahidjo was buried in Senegal. The movement in Cameroon to restore his reputation is gaining support. A sports stadium in Yaoundé has been named in his memory (as a young man he was a soccer player). Plans have been made to remove his remains from Senegal to Cameroon with all appropriate honors.

He was an influential leader in the 1960s sweep of independence in Africa. He faced unique challenges of ethnic and religious diversity, and set the foundation for a multiethnic state with a tradition of religious freedom.

Books by and about Ahmadou Ahidjo

Ahidjo, Ahmadou. *The Political Philosophy of Ahmadou Ahidjo*. Monaco: Paul Bory Publishers, 1968.

Johnson, Willard R. *The Cameroon Federation: Political Integration in a Fragmentary Society*. Princeton, N.J.: Princeton University Press, 1970.

Le Vine, Victor T. *The Cameroons: From Mandate to Independence*. Westport, Conn.: Greenwood Press, 1977.

Takougang, Joseph. "The Nature of Politics in Cameroon." In *The Leadership Challenge in Africa: Cameroon Under Paul Biya*. Trenton, N.J.: Africa World Press, 2004.

Welch, Jr., Claude E. *Dream of Unity: Pan Africanism and Political Unification in West Africa*. Ithaca, N.Y.: Cornell University Press, 1966.

Epilogue

Africa's New Leaders

The sweep of independence that rushed through sub-Saharan, black Africa quickly embraced all of the areas previously colonized by the British, French, and Belgium states. All colonial areas were included in the sweep of the 1960s with the exception of the Portuguese colonial areas, where it occurred in 1975.

The new states of Africa were faced with challenges that are still having an impact on the development of peoples. The scars left by the slave trade and the cruel early days of colonialism have affected the growth of these countries. These facts combined with the pressures of poverty, illiteracy, and disease present in so many of the African countries have held up socioeconomic growth of the black African peoples.

The inherent strength and resiliency of the African peoples, however, have produced strong new leaders as the world enters the third millennium. These more recent leaders assure us that the black African states are assuming their positions of responsibilities in the community of nations.

Nelson Mandela

A primary example is Nelson Mandela, who provided leadership to a country that was a bastion of white supremacy. South Africa was one of the most defiant strongholds of white supremacy in the world. The original political philosophy of apartheid was a political-theological doctrine postulating God-given superiority for the white man. This translated into a devastating economic equation where the white man prospered at the expense of the black man. Margaret and Tom visited the country in 1962 and were overwhelmed with the fear that the sweep of independence would ignite a racial bloodbath when it reached South Africa.

A bloodbath was spared because of the inspiring early leadership of Albert John Luthuli, who was awarded a Nobel Prize in 1960. With great caution and with the assistance of Durban's archbishop, we met privately with Luthuli in 1962, when he was under house arrest. He inspired us with his observation that, despite the distressing situation, he believed a change could occur without a bloodbath.

In many ways, it is astounding that the conciliatory attitude of Luthuli was continued and implemented by Nelson Mandela. Born in 1918, he served twenty-seven years in prison, most of it in isolation on Robben Island. He "turned the other cheek" and never advocated revenge, but rather worked for a multiracial democracy. He served as president of South Africa from 1994 to 1999. The recipient of the Nobel Prize for Peace in 1993, he is now in his nineties and suffering from some of the infirmities of old age. He remains the symbol of racial reconciliation.

Sam Nujoma

Sam Nujoma was the founder and first president of Namibia. Located in southwest Africa, the country has had a stable multiparty democratic government since its founding in 1990. Sam Nujoma provided strong leadership in the preindependence days. We would meet with him when he visited the United Nations advocating independence for his country. Notwithstanding the racial tensions present in southern Africa, Sam Nujoma, like Sylvanus Olympio, advocated and practiced engagement.

A frequent visitor to the United Nations in the preindependence period, Sam Nujoma utilized his time at the organization to make contacts with humanitarian organizations. He was constantly seeking relief supplies for the refugees from Namibia living in nearby Zambia. We put him in contact with Catholic Relief Services, which sent several large shipments of clothing to the Namibian refugee camps.

Popular with the people of Namibia, Sam Nujoma soon gained the title of "Father of the Nation." He offered an avuncular style of leadership during his presidency. As BBC News commentator Franke Jensen correctly said, "The family-man president has managed to maintain stability in the 'rainbow nation.'"

Yoweri Museveni

Uganda, a landlocked country in East Africa, has benefited from the strong leadership of Yoweri Museveni. The country, formally a protectorate of the British, had the great misfortune in the early years of independence of becoming the victim of Idi Amin, who seized power in 1971 and expelled the Indian minority, an important middle class of the country. Around three hundred thousand Ugandans were killed during Amin's reign of terror, which lasted eight years.

Tom served as the U.S. ambassador to Uganda in 1972–73, and we personally witnessed the devastation that the Amin rule brought to the country. Yoweri Museveni seized power in 1986 and in many ways "picked-up the pieces." Within a few years Museveni succeeded in establishing stability that was praised by Western leaders. Political stability has resulted in an increase in the flow of investment capital to Uganda.

Museveni met the challenges of an HIV/AIDS pandemic. In a strong national campaign he significantly reduced the number of victims. His executive style in management was influenced by his military background. These efforts have resulted in some criticism as he is impatient with bureaucratic procedures. With the exception of the problems on the northern Ugandan border, his leadership has won overall praise from European and American leaders.

Paul Kagame

Rwanda, the home of Paul Kagame, who has served as president since 2000, is the recent scene of both tragedy and recovery. This landlocked country, about the size of Maryland, has suffered from two periods of internal strife. Before and immediately after 1962, thousands of Rwandans were killed in the struggle between the two communities, the Tutsis and the Hutus.

A far more horrible situation developed in 1994 when genocide took the lives of eight hundred thousand people, mostly Tutsi and Hutu moderates. Despite these recent catastrophes, the country has now been described by many African experts as a success story. In less than two decades Rwanda has become a model for developing countries. In business, a leading journal, *Fortune,* has praised the country's favorable business climate. Human rights groups cite the rapid rise of women in political spheres. At one point the majority of members of the national legislature were women. The Commonwealth of Nations even admitted Rwanda as a member, an honor given to only one other state not formally a member of the British commonwealth system.

Paul Kagame is responsible for Rwanda being named a success story in Africa. He is now a leading third world advocate of new models for foreign aid, placing great emphasis on developing countries to become self-reliant.

Kagame's dynamic drive for significant improvement in the economy of Rwanda has brought some criticism due to his aggressive style. The results he has achieved, however, in rebuilding the life and economy in a country only recently devastated by genocide are remarkable.

Jakaya Kikwete

Democratic traditions in a pluralist society were firmly established by Julius Nyerere at the founding of Tanzania. He must also be credited with initiating a very strong tradition of freedom from corruption. This has been continued by his successors. Jakaya Kikwete is the fourth (and current) president of the Republic of Tanzania.

Julius Nyerere, a Catholic, emphasized the importance of religious freedom in the founding of the new state on the East African coast. President Kikwete, a follower of Islam, is continuing the now strong tradition of religious freedom.

Born in 1950, Kikwete rose steadily through civil and military positions to become president in 2005. During his previous service as minister of foreign affairs he undertook the difficult task of resolving the brutal violence in the Great Lakes region of the east Congo and Burundi. He is one of the increasing number of new leaders in Africa who are setting high standards for engagement not only providing stable leadership for the country, but also promoting peaceful solutions to the conflicts of the region.

These five leaders are characteristic of the new leadership in black Africa. They, like their predecessors, in the sweep of independence in the 1960s, faced the consequences of societies still plagued by poverty, illiteracy, and disease. These five leaders of civil society have provided stable leadership so that their countries have a recognized presence in the world community.

The black leadership in the Catholic Church is also very impressive. When Tom was living in Ethiopia in 1957 the overwhelming majority of bishops in black Africa were white. Recognizing the importance of elevating to leadership native African clergy, many white African bishops resigned and consequently were replaced by native African priests. Now there are over five hundred African bishops providing leadership to the Catholic Church in Africa. In 1960, there was only a handful. The increase in African leadership also matches the increase in the number of African Catholics. In 1960, there were approximately 22 million; that number increased in 2005 to 159 million.

The growth of the Catholic Church in Africa has not been without challenges, but the leadership is stable and effective. Both on the governmental side, as well as in the church, the black African people have provided competent and dedicated leadership.

Appendix 1

Protestants and Catholics Speak to Portuguese Leaders, 1961

National Council of Churches Press Release
June 5, 1961

More than eighty prominent Protestant and Roman Catholic clergy and laymen in the United States and Canada have appealed to Portugal to bring a halt to the bloodshed in Angola, West Africa.

In an open letter to "The President and People of Portugal," today they expressed their concern that the situation in the Portuguese territory "threatens to explode into a war of extermination between the Portuguese and Africans."

The writers urged President (Rear Admiral) Americo Tomaz to set up a consultation of representatives of his government and Angolan leaders "to seek a reasonable solution" to end the indiscriminate killings.

Recent reports to the Africa Committee of the National Council of Churches indicate that at least 1,000 whites and 8,000 Angolans have been killed to date. Some estimates of African casualties run as high as 20,000, the Rev. Theodore L. Tucker, committee secretary, stated in a covering letter to Protestant leaders requesting their signatures.

Among the U.S. signatories to the appeal, in addition to Dr. Tucker, are Dr. Thomas P. Melady, chairman, Africa Committee, Catholic Association for International Peace; Dr. Robert G. Goheen, president of Princeton University; Father John LaFarge, editor emeritus of *America*; former Sen. Joseph C. O'Mahoney; and A. Philip Randolph, international president, Brotherhood of Sleeping Car Porters.

Names of prominent Canadians include: The Rev. R. M. Bennett, secretary, Department of Overseas Missions, Canadian Council of Churches; the Rev. T. E. Floyd Honey, secretary, Board of Missions, United Church of Canada; and Mrs. Hugh D. Taylor, Women's Missionary Society, United Church of Canada.

Declaring that it is the obligation of any state to control rioting and armed manifestations, they deplored the violent reaction in Angola "which has carried suppression to excessive lengths." Thousands of Angolans have been reported killed in indiscriminate reprisals, they said, and warned that the reestablishment of controls by the government will be "an empty victory" without redress of grievances.

The message also quoted the recent pastoral letter from Roman Catholic bishops in Angola in which they condemned the killings by the rebels but supported their "legitimate and just aspirations" for justice and social betterment.

The U.S. and Canadian spokesmen expressed their hopes that the newly appointed Portuguese Minister for Overseas Portugal, Dr. Adriano Moreira, will take immediate steps to restore racial harmony.

"We welcome his announcement," they said, "that administrative and legislative measures will be put into force immediately to eliminate social injustices."

Stating that these efforts can only succeed through consultations with representatives of the African people, the message concluded: "We appeal to you, Mr. President, and to the people of Portugal, to initiate this process of discussion."

Calling the situation "an opportunity for the Portuguese people to rise to greatness," the letter appealed for an effective and just solution for all concerned.

Appendix 2

Senghor's Address on the Civilization of the Universe

Address by His Excellency, Léopold Sédar Senghor President, the Republic of Senegal Fordham University November 2, 1961

In my own country, the country of the man who comes to visit you today, to know (*connaître*) means to be born with, to be born anew (*con-naître*) and signifies also to die in order to be reborn. I do not bring you anything else except the readiness and humility of a very ancient people, who have known the vicissitudes of history, but who have never lost faith in themselves and in the future of mankind. This is then the message of our universities of black Africa, which are a school of life.

To this readiness and humility we have added the method of Europe. This means that we have rejected and that we will continue to reject isolation, even a splendid isolation. We must admit that our relations with Europe have not always been smooth, but these difficulties prove that there has been a contact between two civilizations. It is true also that Europe has

destroyed in our countries many values worthy of consideration, but it was in order to bring us other values to replace our
own. We have transformed European values into complements
of our own values, meaning that we have stamped them with
the seal of black Africa. By so doing we have remained faithful
to ourselves and to history, and we have accomplished this without creating among us any complexes. The reality of history is
constituted by the presence in the United States of America of
17 million Negroes, who came from Africa with sweat on their
brows, rhythm in their hearts, strength in their arms. These
Negroes have left their mark in the life of the most powerful
nation in modern times. Nowhere else could one be more con-
scious of this historical reality than here at Fordham, and the
best proof is to be found on the shelves of your library, which
display, side by side, books on the French Revolution and on the
American Revolution. A momentous fact occurred in the first
ten years of your University, of great importance for the countries of black Africa. The abolition of slavery in Europe took
place seven years after the foundation of St. John's College by
Archbishop Hughes. A few years before, the American Society
for the Defense of the Black Race had decided to transplant
on the African coast former slaves to whom freedom had been
restored. Thus was born the Republic of Liberia, a neighboring
country, with whom the Republic of Senegal maintains relations
of friendship and brotherly love, within an association known
today as the Monrovia Group.

Historians have underlined the importance of the Act of
April 27, 1848. It marked a turning point in the evolution of the
world even though it was only the result of a generous impulse

of a rather narrow-minded bourgeoisie. The importance of this Act lies essentially in the idea that it created in this return to "normal life." This was certainly not a surprise for the Negroes of America who, for many years, through their Negro blues and spirituals had kept alive what the poet Aimé Césaire has called "the bitter taste for liberty."

The revolutionaries of 1848 were not, indeed, political men. They were poets. This explains their vision of a generous world arising in a spirit of brotherhood. They were the first to dream of a total liberation of man. It is true also that the revolutionary poets of 1848 were the brothers of the tribunes of 1793. The teaching of history is a means of asserting the possibilities of the future while remaining in touch with the past. Above all, it makes it possible to cast on daily events the light of past experiments. Archbishop Hughes had understood that lesson, endowed, as he was, with such a keen vision of the future.

We are then, ladies and gentlemen of Fordham, at a crossroad. In New York, in this city which people carelessly have called heartless, your mission is to maintain an island of hope. Your University, as I have said, enjoys an international reputation. It is above all a place where men of different races, different countries, different philosophies, may meet each other. This was also the vision of Archbishop Hughes — to start from one's own data and to accede to a deeper knowledge of other continents, of other people. Such is the method that Negro-Africans apply in approaching the world. It is a sign and an expression of readiness.

At Fordham, you are the dispensers of science, that is to say, of knowledge. You teach law, which is a method to govern society; education, which is the art to raise children; pharmacy, which is the preservation of health. You teach the arts and sciences, which are manifestations of the genius of man; philosophy, which is the rule of life; finally, the sciences, which are means of investigation and discovery. You have understood your mission, which, is to arm these young men and women for the struggle which is life. Your vocation consists in training them to be responsible and open-minded men and women.

Turning now to you, students of Fordham University, I cannot resist the temptation to quote these verses, which you know so well, of the poet Walt Whitman, the most powerful poet of America, by his inspiration, his vision, and his strength. In the manner of the African patriarchs, Walt Whitman said:

> I announce myriads of youths, beautiful, gigantic, sweet-
> blooded,
> I announce a race of splendid and savage old men.

Young men and young women of America, you have the good fortune to be able to face a world devoted to the philosophy of the absurd carrying as your viaticum the hope sung by Walt Whitman. For it is, indeed, a matter of hope. Whitman teaches you a way of being, a way of life. Poet, he is solidly rooted in his soil but he gazes upon and embraces the entire world. He was a man in a state of readiness. He was a man faithful in friendship, and his eyes were resolutely turned toward the future.

The greatest lyric poet of the United States of America has given us a splendid lesson in humanism, which is expressed in the following verses:

And what I assume, you shall assume,
For every atom belongs to me, as good belongs to you.

Such is the message that a poet who is not only a poet of America, but a poet of the world, transmits to you. It expresses a humanistic vision of the world. It announces an ideal. It is now your duty, drawing upon your youthful enthusiasm, to keep this ideal alive. You are now responsible for a world which has been shaped by your predecessors. You have traditions to be maintained, dreams to be realized, a vision to be extended. If your predecessors were kind men, you must be kind men also, but with a strong will. You have been trained in traditions based on the respect of the human person. In this University, you will learn to be modest and to work, according to tested methods. You will leave Fordham proud possessors of enviable academic titles; but these titles will not help you in resolving all the problems which will be presented to you. Your academic titles will give you the ability to face these problems, but their solution will be dependent upon the way in which you will face them, I mean in your method.

What now will be these problems which will be presented to you, and which will call urgently for an answer? They will be the problems of a man, who, in a world of science and of techniques, is seeking his balance. Armed with the knowledge which is now imparted to you by your eminent masters, you will have to find your true selves and realize all your potentialities.

Archives of Fordham University

President Senghor speaking at Fordham University in 1961.

You will need more than courage, more than perspicacity. You will need to remain in a state of readiness, as we are in the Negro-African tradition. You will have to tame a world in the manner of the first men. Needless to say, oceans and forests will no longer constitute obstacles for you. But you will face harsh realities. You will think that you are in another world when the problem will be to conquer hunger, ignorance, disease, poverty in a world which seems to be so well provided. It will be difficult for you to think that, at a time when automation reigns supreme and when the most varied foods are produced by machines, in other parts of this planet, other men seek their livelihood by the strength of their arms, with the most primitive tools. But you will not be surprised by the hope of these millions of men who know full well that they are backward and yet refuse to yield to pessimism, refuse to be discouraged. You will not be surprised because Walt Whitman will already have told you:

> A worship new I sing,
> You captains, voyagers, explorers, yours,
> You engineers, you architects, machinists, yours,
> You, not for trade or transportation only,
> But in God's name, and for thy sake O soul.

But people of Fordham University, you are being taught, in this very place, that you won't be alone in the world which awaits you. In black Africa, young people like yourselves share the same preoccupations, the same concern. These young people also are hungry and thirsty for knowledge. They know full well that they must bring their contribution to build the civilization of the universal, which will be the work of all, or shall not be. Therefore, the will of the young people of Africa is to start from the original foundation of Negro-African civilization, enlightened and enriched by the contributions of Europe and to meet you at the appointed time. The skeptics will say that this is an impossible ambition, but it is a human ambition, at the measure of Africa, at the measure of the world, which will be built tomorrow.

Like yourselves, the young people of black Africa are in the process of preparing their arms, of forming their minds in the disciplines which now govern the world. They have a keen consciousness of their "situation." Living in a country which is now in the process of being developed, their action has a double meaning; to follow closely the present reality and to look into the future. By so doing, they will have remained faithful to the tradition of their people. Our young people know that it is impossible for them to remain idle, apart from the great movement of history. They know that nature can be tamed, that the means offered by a technical civilization can be of great help to them. The tasks which confront them are, indeed, staggering. But from the education of children to the creation of a great road system, the process is essentially the same. No one will speak henceforth of promethean projects, but what is being achieved now in the fully developed countries thanks to scientific methods and technical means deserves to retain our attention.

Yet, the real originality of this revolution lies elsewhere. From the spark created by the confrontation of two civilizations, the young people of Africa have drawn a flame which will light their way. This process presupposes not only a necessary return to the original sources, but also an opening on the world outside, particularly on Europe and her daughter, America. Europe is proud to call herself the daughter of reason and, by a dialectical method, she has tackled the problems of her evolution. For a long time, she has imposed her views on the rest of the world. On this last point, she has erred. By that, I mean that the triumph of European reason has been harmful to Europe, because it has prevented Europe from becoming aware that other forms of reasoning may exist elsewhere. The Negro-African reason is also dialectical since it is based on a communication, on a form of knowledge obtained through sympathy. If the European is a bird of prey, the Negro-African remains earthly, that is to say, all senses. Aimé Césaire has said of him that he is porous to all the inspirations of the world. These two attitudes are not contradictory, but rather complement each other, and from their union, the civilization of tomorrow, the New Man will be born. The contribution of Africa will be to bring into the evolution of the world an element of love, since love is also a confrontation of two attitudes. Having started from our own philosophy, we have approached without apprehension the philosophy of Europe. Without apprehension, indeed, yet with real humility. Our own vocation is to demonstrate that, among the European methods of constructing the world there is room for other values, the values in which all people believe. One will not be surprised then to learn that our own experience leads to a constructive critique of European reason.

European reason is abstract mainly because it has willfully forsaken spiritual values. Instead of abstraction we have chosen another principle, a principle of reunion, oriented toward a complete communion of all people. In order to be really constructive, this principle must rely on the spiritual forces of man. Our attitude is then one of conciliation between the external and the internal realities of the world. The African socialist way, which was born on the banks of the Senegal River, is nothing else but this lucidness and this love before nature, this courage to face the other through sympathy. Such will be the contribution of our continent to the civilization of the universal. Then a new race of men will appear on the earth, a race of pioneers, full of endeavor, "playing the very game of the world." They will be men without prejudices, and men who "will give light wings to reason." It is this new race which Walt Whitman announced in the following verses:

> A world of new primitives has risen with
> perspectives of incessant and increased life:
> A musty and active race is installing and
> organizing itself.
> I sing of a new cult, I dedicate it to you
> —Captain, Navigator, Explorer—
> To you, Engineer, to you, Architect, to you,
> Machine maker.
> Come to me, I wish to create the indissoluble continent,
> I wish to make the most magnificent race
> upon which the sun has ever shone,
> I wish to make admirable, magnetic countries
> With brotherly love
> which lasts as long as the life of the comrades,
> I wish to plant brotherly love as strong as

the trees which bear the flowers of
America and the shores of the Great Lakes
and which cover the prairie.
I wish that the cities become inseparable.
Their arms around the neck of one another....

Distinguished professors, students of Fordham University, a poet has shown you the way, the way of hope and of courage. Walt Whitman, the poet of America thus meets Archbishop Hughes, founder of your University, the sages of Africa and of Asia, the masters of sciences of Europe. Man is saved since his hope has been maintained. We are now, all of us, of different features, color, languages, customs, stirred and carried by the same movement of life. We are on our way toward the world of tomorrow, the world of the civilization of the universal.

Khama's Address
on Racial Reconciliation

Address by the Honorable Seretse Khama, Prime Minister of Bechuanaland, on the occasion of his receiving the LL.D (honoris causa) on October 25, 1965, at Fordham University, New York

Reverend President, Trustees, Members of the Faculty, friends, and students, I consider it a very great honor to address you today and to have been awarded the degree of doctor of laws (honoris causa). When I heard the distinguished list of men and women who have been awarded degrees here before, I realized how privileged I am to have my name added to that list, and I hope that I will prove worthy of the honor you have bestowed upon me. Fordham University has a great and well-deserved reputation, and I am proud to be associated with Fordham. You may be interested to know that I am the first Motswana to be honored in this way by any university, and it is therefore an honor that is appreciated by the people of Bechuanaland as well as myself. When one considers that only sixty years ago a colonial administrator of Bechuanaland could write — "it is too soon as yet to be able to judge of the success likely to attend the teaching of a Motswana, but judging from what we see of him and his works he does not appear to display any particular ability" — I am delighted that the trustees of Fordham were able to take a more charitable view of this particular Motswana by considering him worthy of this honor.

Reverend President, there are few subjects about which I feel able and qualified to address this distinguished convocation, but perhaps after seven months as prime minister of Bechuanaland I should be able to give you some idea of the problems that beset a young nation and to explain a little of our plans and aspirations for the future.

Bechuanaland is indeed a young country. Its boundaries as they stand now were demarcated only seventy years ago, and we achieved internal self-government in March of this year. As you may know we expect to have independence by September 30, 1966.

Independence has been our goal for a number of years, and I and my people have endeavored to work for it in a responsible manner, realizing that while the administration of our own country was a right to which we were entitled, it was a responsibility for which we had to be fully prepared. Bechuanaland has not figured greatly in the newspapers of the world because we have worked for independence peacefully and responsibly. However, I must admit that I believe that the problems that face us at independence are certainly greater than have faced most other colonial territories at a similar stage, and however successfully we may have utilized our national resources, we will fall short of what we require for an independent nation in many respects.

For the sake of simplicity it is possible to describe our problems as falling into three main categories. The first of these arises out of our geographical position in Africa in that we are virtually surrounded by countries which have quite different policies from our own; the second, and probably most fundamental, is that Bechuanaland is one of the poorest countries, on a relatively poor continent; and thirdly, and arising out of the first two, we lack adequate numbers of educated Botswana to administer and develop our country.

My ideal is to establish in Bechuanaland a democratic state, which must also be completely nonracial and unified. I cannot contemplate a future for Bechuanaland with separate representations for different racial groups, as with second-class citizenship and imbalanced representation one cannot provide fully for the rights and interests of all sections of the community. Nor by such a system could we create a unified nation in Bechuanaland. Many do say and will say that this is an experiment that is bound to fail. Many base such a view on pure racial prejudice. Some base it on mere practical considerations, and they argue that one cannot justifiably expose the wealth and high standards of living of the more developed white section of the community to the whims and prejudices of the untutored African majority of the people, and that it is wrong to expose those minority sections who are at present best able to produce the wealth, technical knowledge, and general ability, to the political caprices of African majorities.

These are the arguments that our neighbors in South Africa used to support their policies divergent from our own. We stand virtually alone in southern Africa in our own belief that a nonracial society can work now, and there are those among our neighbors who would be only too delighted to see our experiment fail.

We have I believe made some real progress in creating a nonracial and harmonious society in Bechuanaland during the last few years. It is a source of pleasure to me that in our elections in March it was quite apparent that Europeans in Bechuanaland were prepared to and did vote in constituencies where all the candidates were Africans. Conversely in one constituency where 95 percent of the electorate were Africans, it was a European who took 85 percent of the vote, where his two opponents were Africans. These are healthy signs that our people are tolerant and sensible enough to discount the accident of a man's color and concentrate on his ability and usefulness to his country. Further, all our schools are now integrated, and those who scoffed a few years ago at the suggestion that we would be able to maintain standards of education and therefore removed their children have now in many cases accepted this integration and have returned their children to the nonracial schools. I would not like to suggest to you that integration in Bechuanaland has been a simple or even completely successful operation, but I believe we have shown that people of difference races and of different backgrounds, who only a few years ago lived in completely separate societies, have found that when they make the effort to come together and are prepared to exercise tolerance for each other's way of life, they can gain greatly from each other's experience. We have still a long way to go before we can say that our nonracial society has succeeded and is completely accepted, but our experiment must succeed in Bechuanaland or our neighbors will have a sound case for showing that apartheid is the answer.

The advocates of apartheid in the Republic of South Africa enjoy making political capital out of the fact that the African in the Republic enjoys a higher standard of living than his brother in Bechuanaland. And at present the case is a difficult one to answer. Bechuanaland is not going to survive on a moral sense of superiority by virtue of the freedom of its people; it must also have an economically prosperous people. Freedom is all very well, but it will not fill the stomachs of the Botswana. I think it may surprise you to know that my country, which is roughly the size of Texas and has a population of over half a million, until quite recently existed on an annual budget of about $1 million. I wonder how many yards of tarmac you could lay on New York streets for that sum. It is only during the last ten years that we have been able to raise money for development, and it is hardly surprising that we have been unable to effect all the development programs we require.

Bechuanaland does need development capital to institute essential programs for our cattle industry, for our agriculture, for our water development, and for education and social services. For these programs we require very substantial sums of money in the form of limited free grants and soft loans, and it has been made quite apparent to me that we cannot expect the British government to finance all our requirements. In the past, as a dependent British protectorate all our development funds have been supplied by Britain, but as you well know the British economy is experiencing considerable difficulties, and it seems most unlikely that our grant aid will be increased, as we require in the future. The problem is therefore quite simply a question of to whom do we turn for these funds. It is distressing, but understandable, to note that many countries get assistance only if they become an international problem; if they become a pawn in the differences between East and West. It is not my ambition, when we achieve independence, to sit on the fence between East and West and to place Bechuanaland at the disposal of the highest bidder. But as a politician, who believes that the economic development of his country and the prosperity of his people are among the most important goals he must pursue, it is my duty to seek and find the assistance that my country requires.

I know that the more prosperous countries of the world are already a little tired of the large number of new nations which attempt to hold them as ransom, but I would prefer to approach those nations whose policies and ideals are the same as my own. However, it is the harsh reality of politics that if I cannot meet the needs of my people, they will turn to my political opponents, who already operate with funds supplied by Communist countries and who have promises of further assistance should they come to power in Bechuanaland. Nonetheless, at present I believe that I do represent the interests and loyalties of the vast majority of Botswana, as in March this year my party was returned with the support of over 80 percent of the vote, and holds twenty-eight of the thirty-one elected seats in our Legislative Assembly. However, when one considers that the first year of my government has been marked by the most disastrous famine the country has experienced in thirty-five years and 20 percent of the people are classified as destitute, you will understand that our introduction to politics has not been an easy one.

In a country as backward as my own, which has so many needs, it is difficult to give absolute priority to any particular form of development. But certainly one of our greatest needs is to develop our educational system so that we may train Botswana for the country's administration. If you will forgive me I should like to give you a few statistics as they illustrate our pressing difficulties. At present almost 50 percent of our population has received no education whatsoever; of children who are now between the ages of five and twenty only one-third attend school — and this is not because of any reluctance to attend school, but because the schools are full and in many cases overcrowded. Of our teachers less than 50 percent are qualified. As an illustration of this last point, in one of our primary schools in 1962 a teacher with only three years schooling himself was found to be teaching a class in the fifth year of the primary course.

Throughout the country we have only 6 secondary schools with a total enrollment of 1,036 pupils. We require at least another 400 qualified teachers and 1,000 new classrooms to meet our current needs, and we have 2,291 in the country of which a substantial number are posts held by expatriates, posts that could be held by Botswana if they had the qualifications. But we are producing only 216 passes a year with the minimum qualifications of a secondary school certificate. You will understand therefore our position is hardly a happy one in the basic lower levels of education, and there is an equally pressing need for us to expand our postsecondary vocational and university

training. At present there are 67 Botswana training in universities and colleges abroad, 6 of these here in the United States,
and I am happy to say 5 more have recently been awarded
scholarships in this country.

In spite of our ever present shortage of funds we have,
perhaps optimistically, prepared plans involving a capital expen-
diture of some $5 million to improve our existing secondary
schools and to build another, to offer courses for unqualified
teachers, to build an agriculture training school, and to develop
our only vocational training college. These are programs for
which we do not have sufficient funds to implement, but if the
shortfall should become available, we should be able during the
next ten years to train sufficient Botswana for most of the posts
we require below the specialist level.

However, I would not like to give the impression that the
people of Bechuanaland are merely waiting for the rest of the
world to come to their assistance. We do have a thriving Community Development Department, which is directing self-help
programs. In a country where the per capita income is as low as
$40 per annum, we have built many classrooms with volunteer
labor. During the last few years my own tribe has built no less
than forty classrooms by their own efforts, and there is a volun-
tary educational levy in some areas. Botswana are pathetically
eager to have education, but last year we had only three hundred secondary school places for seventeen hundred applicants
with the requisite qualifications.

If we do not succeed in educating our own people we will
either have to allow expatriates to continue to fill important
posts in the administration and cause bitter discontent among

our own people, or else by placing untrained Botswana in posts they are unqualified to hold, we will allow the standards of administration to fall and the economic development of the country to stagnate. If this is the choice my vision of a harmonious and prosperous nonracial state will never materialize, and the critics of our policies will be justified. However, I have great faith that others will find that my hopes are worthy of support, and that in the course of time we will create in Bechuanaland the society we want.

Reverend President, I hope I have not occupied your time unduly. A favorite pastime of my people is to stand up in the *kgotla,* our council chamber in Bechuanaland, and to assert "I have nothing to say" and then proceed to say nothing over a period of time that would excite . . . a filibustering American Congressman.

Rev. President, quite apart from the great honor that Fordham has done to me this day you have given me the opportunity to give a little publicity to the present state of my country and of our needs for the future. If today I have been able to awaken interest in my country I am even more in the debt of Fordham University.

About the Authors

Thomas Patrick Melady has had a career in three fields: diplomacy, higher education, and public affairs.

He served in four diplomatic posts: U.S. ambassador to Burundi, U.S. ambassador to Uganda, senior advisor to the U.S. Delegation to the United Nations, and U.S. ambassador to the Holy See.

His experience in higher education includes service as executive vice president of St. Joseph's University in Philadelphia and as president of Sacred Heart University in Fairfield, Connecticut. He was also assistant U.S. secretary of education for post-secondary education during President Reagan's first term. He served on the faculties of St. John's, Fordham, George Washington, and Seton Hall Universities.

As an active participant in public affairs, Ambassador Melady was president and chief executive officer of the Connecticut Public and Economic council. He is also the author of sixteen other books and numerous articles. Twenty-nine universities have conferred their honorary doctorates on Dr. Melady, and five foreign states and the Holy See have also awarded him their high honors.

Ambassador Melady is a Knight in obedience of the Sovereign Military Order of Malta and is vice delegate in the

United States for the Sacred Military Constantinian Order of St. George. He has also served on the National Board of Directors of the National Conference of Christians and Jews and the International League for Human Rights.

He received his B.A. degree from Duquesne University and his M.A. and Ph.D.: degrees (in international relations, government, and economics) from the Catholic University of America. He and his wife, the former Margaret Badum, have two adult daughters.

Ambassador Melady is now professor and senior diplomat in residence at the Institute of World Politics in Washington, D.C., and serves on the boards and committees of several nonprofit organizations.

Margaret Badum Melady is president of Melady Associates, a firm specializing in public affairs and educational consulting. Dr. Melady has a rich background in university teaching and administration, corporate management, and global communication. From 1997 to 2003, Dr. Melady served as president of the American University of Rome, Italy's first American independent degree-granting university. As director of Corporate Communications of United Illuminating, a public utility company, Dr. Melady was responsible for external and internal communications including advertising and media relations. At Chesebrough-Pond's, Dr. Melady directed a nationwide program in state governmental affairs. She was the first woman promoted to an executive position in public affairs at Stauffer Chemical Company, where she worked in both public relations and governmental affairs.

Dr. Melady produced and moderated her own radio programs and has appeared on many radio and television programs. Dr. Melady received a master's degree from Seton Hall University and a doctorate in social science from the Gregorian University of Rome. She is the author of three books on political and cultural studies: *Léopold Sédar Senghor: Rhythm and Reconciliation* (Seton Hall University Press); *Rhetoric of Pope John Paul II: The Pastoral Visit* (Praeger); *Poesie Vivante II* (Louvain University Press), plus two books co-authored with her husband.

Index

Numbers in **_bold italics_** indicate photos.